Life on the Old Farm

Life on the Old Farm

Tom Quinn

David and Charles

A DAVID & CHARLES BOOK
Copyright © David & Charles Limited, 2011

David & Charles is an F+W Media, Inc. company
4700 East Galbraith Road
Cincinnati, OH 45236

First published in the UK in 2011
Text copyright © Tom Quinn 2011

Tom Quinn has asserted his right to be identified
as author of this work in accordance with the
Copyright, Designs and Patents Act, 1988.

Material from this book has been previously published in *Tales of the
Old Country Farmers* published by David & Charles Ltd, 1995.

A catalogue record for this book is available from the British Library.

ISBN 13: 978-1-4463-0065-7
ISBN 10: 1-4463-0065-X

Printed in Finland by Bookwell Oy
for David & Charles
Brunel House   Newton Abbot   Devon

Commissioning Editor: Neil Baber
Editor: Verity Muir
Senior Designer: Victoria Marks
Production Controller: Bev Richardson

David & Charles publish high quality books on a
wide range of subjects.

For more great book ideas visit:
www.rubooks.co.uk

ACKNOWLEDGEMENTS

I owe a great debt of gratitude to the farmers whose memories lie at the heart of this book. All put up cheerfully with my endless demands for more information and with my limitless capacity to drink tea.

A complex illustrated book like this actually has very little to do with the author once the typescript has left his hands, but that is the moment at which a number of other people – particularly editors and illustrators – have to sort out the business of words and pictures and knitting them together. With that in mind I would like to thank Philip Murphy, who drew the pictures, and Verity Muir at David & Charles.

I would also like to thank the following individuals and institutions: Harry Robson, J.T. Lovett-Turner, Arthur Court, E. Peter Day, David Powell, Mr Avery, George Pemberley, May Constance, Mrs M.I. Greenway, John Williams-Davies, J.R. Hughes, Gerald Pendry, T. Erwyd Howells, Blanaid Salkeld, Robin Belben, J.A. Tomkins, H. Oswald Harrison, George Gadwell Hall, Karen Warren of Pipe Dreams, Sarah Storey, Barbara Thompson, Debbie Fischer, Miss L. Plummer, Sarah Doak, E.D. Westall, Louise Davies, Nicky Bird, Jane Smith, Karen Warren, Charlotte Wadham, Emma, Katy, James, Alex and Joe, The British Library and The Time Machine.

Contents

INTRODUCTION

A time-traveller from the Middle Ages wandering the fields of England during the first three decades of this century would have been astonished at the great, laborious steam engines that helped with the harvest in many areas; but in almost every other respect he would have recognised immediately agricultural practices and traditions little changed since the close of the Dark Ages. Horses had replaced oxen, it is true, and the great fields divided into strips had gone, but the countryside was still a place where mechanisation had made only minor inroads. The steady pace of life was dictated by the horse; animals were driven to market along the ancient drovers' roads, and tiny fields surrounded by well-grown hedges dominated much of the landscape.

At the beginning of this century the countryside was a much more densely populated place than it is today: a lowland farmer might employ a shepherd, a team of horsemen and their assistants, a cowman, milkmaids and odd-job men. All had tied cottages, and although they often lived at or beneath the poverty line, they had sufficient finances to fuel a local economy of shops, pubs, blacksmiths, wheelwrights and farriers, which now has all but disappeared.

Our medieval time-traveller would also have recognised the local nature of life in a society where few people travelled anywhere outside their immediate environment, and if they did travel at all, it was on foot. In the pubs, clay pipes were still smoked beneath the gloomy light thrown by candles and oil lamps, and the dust rose in summer from the winding, unmade roads.

It was World War II that accelerated a process of change in the countryside that had begun in the Great War. Change had to come because, at a time of national crisis, it was essential that farmers should use the latest chemicals and technology in order to produce the maximum amount of food. After that there was no going back.

With the advent of the mass-produced motor car, tractors and combine harvesters, and also the development of chemical fertilisers, the last great movement from the land to the towns and cities took place. The heavy horses that had powered the farming world vanished within a few years, along with most of the farmworkers' jobs, and by the late 1950s and early 1960s, many villages had become mere dormitories for the towns; men who might once have worked on the land now drove away from the village each day to work in factories and offices. Today our medieval time-traveller would find himself lost in an unfamiliar world, a rural world so dominated by tractor and car that it more nearly reflects the values of the town.

The old values and way of life may have entirely vanished, but many of the men who knew that horse-driven world at first-hand were still alive in the 1980s when much of the research for this book was conducted. They were by then in extreme old age but their memories of the distant past were still remarkably vivid and it is these memories of a vanished world – a world that links us directly to our medieval ancestors – that are recorded here. Although they record some of the most attractive aspects of what was essentially a pre-industrial English countryside, they also include memories of hardship and deprivation, and are therefore recollections that should act as a caution to those who over-idealise the rustic past.

The farmers who agreed to talk to me include men from widely differing social backgrounds; at one extreme there is the gentleman farmer who inherited everything, and at the other the labourer who scraped together enough money at last to take a lease on his own farm.

Most of us have an image of the countryside that is based on nostalgia for some rustic idyll; but if this book has any merit it lies in the fact that it re-creates the past as far as possible as it was, and not as we might have liked it to be. Nevertheless, for all its realism, this portrait of the past is, I hope, both a tribute to those who once worked the land and an attempt to preserve the best of it from the long oblivion of history.

TOM QUINN – 2011

WILL CONSTANCE

SCOLE, NORFOLK

*W*ill Constance was ninety-two when I interviewed him. He had spent his life in one of the most traditionally agricultural parts of the country: Norfolk. Until the building of the M11, Norfolk, like most of East Anglia, was cut off from the main north-south road and rail routes that brought change and development to other parts of the country. As late as the mid-1960s many remote Norfolk villages were still served by delivery vans pulled by horses and even today the smaller Norfolk roads still twist and turn as they did centuries ago, and every few yards along the tiniest by-road there is, it seems, a village, a hamlet, or one or two isolated houses. And in Norfolk almost every dwelling-place seems to be at least two or three hundred years old, for this is a deeply conservative county where traditions change slowly, and land is passed on carefully from father to son.

Although he was frail and confined to a nursing home when I met him, Will's conversation still sparkled with the memory of former times: of the dusty roads, of horses, and of travellers covering a few miles a day across the lonely fields. But as Will emphasised in his broad Norfolk accent, the countryside was a busy place in his youth, where every farm employed dozens of men, and where instead of the endless arable acres of the modern landscape, farmers grew crops *and* kept animals.

'I was born in 1904 in Scole and I left school at twelve years old, but I was on the farm milking the cows every day from the time I was about ten. Every farm had at least a few cows then. I worked at Rose Farm at Scole when I left school – that would have been about 1916.'

Will was eager to be exact as to seasons, times and places in the past, but his memory was excellent and he pinned down the main events of his early life with enviable precision; some memories were sad, some happy, but most evoked the simple drudgery of a vanished way of life.

'The owner of Rose Farm died in 1922 and I had to move on. You just moved, then, in those circumstances, just got up and left; there was no dole, no social security, no redundancy money. But by then I was a pretty good ploughman. I'd learned to plough two horses side by side, which is the way we did it in Norfolk, and we used a two-furrow plough. At the ploughing time we were up at six o'clock every day, which is hard on a young boy; but we knew nothing else and got used to it, I suppose. So, we fed the horses first, on chaff and corn ground up and mashed together. That was in the stable, but when we turned them out we fed them hay which was put in the iron ricks for them. At night they were turned out into a walled yard which isn't done any more and I don't know why we did it then. But they were always put in the yard rather than in the field or kept in their stalls.

'I would calculate that in the Scole area there would have been four horses and four men to every one hundred acres of land. That's a lot of men and horses. And you imagine those numbers going right across Norfolk and probably Suffolk, too – you can imagine how many people there were in the countryside. Not like now, where each farm is lucky if it has one man, and everyone else gets in a car and dashes off to the nearest town to work. The countryside is empty today, compared to what it was when I was a young man, anyway.'

Every point was emphasised with a wave of Will's great gnarled hands, the hands of a man who had spent virtually every moment of his working life on the land. Horses had been his great love and he was keen to describe exactly how the horseman's day was organised because, as he said, 'we shan't see them no more'.

'After feeding the horses at six o'clock we'd have our own breakfast in the house – we'd never feed before the horses – and then it'd be time to tackle up. We had different kinds of harness for different jobs. Mostly they'd be leather, of course, but for ploughing we put chains on. I suppose the extra weight helped, although the nature of ploughing depends on the nature of the land. On the right kind of land the horses can walk away with it; on heavy clay land, though, they'd be all of a tremble, and winded halfway up a field. Often they'd stop halfway, and they'd be shaking and blowing, and you'd have to let them rest then. It was hard work even for a great strong horse on these lands. Hard work for the man, too, in all weathers, perhaps with only a sack over his shoulders to keep the rain off and miles to walk behind that plough in a day. Only on light land could you plough an acre a day; on heavy land you'd be put to it to do half or three-quarters, and a man walked fourteen miles with his horses to plough one acre. It was hard work, but I never thought much of it because it was what I had to do. You just had to keep walking and you didn't think much about anything as you went along.

'Mind you, if you weren't skilled at it, your arms would be aching from holding the plough and trying to keep an eye on the horses and keeping straight and level at the same time. A good man would hardly touch the handles or the horses; they'd be a real team and know what they were about, with the horses turning on the headland at a word from the ploughman, and he'd be as straight as a die up the field.'

The skill of the ploughman was a great thing in Norfolk when the horse still reigned supreme, and men would travel miles to enter a ploughing match or to compete against a known champion. Ploughing matches were partly a chance to test one's skill against all comers, but they were also important social occasions, as Will recalled.

'Ploughing matches were a great thing round here, here and all over Norfolk. They were judged by men we called "stickers", who got the name because they carried sticks to mark the furrows. In a drawing match you'd draw one furrow only and the stickers would judge you on that, not on a whole field.

'We used old Shire horses when I was young. They were fine to work with, but in the 1920s they were gradually replaced by Suffolk Punches. Now they really were powerful great animals, though good-tempered, most of them. They were also cleaner than the old Shire horse, which was all hair, and if you didn't keep his hairy legs cleaned regularly he got all sorts of problems and went lame. And in the field while he

worked he could get so bogged down with mud that he almost couldn't move, and we'd have to stop in the middle of the field to hack the mud off him to keep him going. So the Suffolk Punch was bound to take over. Yes, they were a big improvement.'

Ploughing was just one part of the horses' work: there was also carting; harrowing and sowing, though these tasks were less arduous than ploughing, as was hoeing which was also done with horses.

'We used horses to hoe the corn when it had just come up; with horse-hoeing, the man led with the horse coming behind. The main crops in my youth were wheat, barley and oats, and oats were very important because we used them for feed for the cows, sheep and horses. We also grew beans and peas. Today, of course, the farmers grow what the European Union tells them to grow and nothing else, and there's little skill in it. Plenty of chemicals, plenty of machines and that's it; not much skill at all. And not much effort either, though I suppose that has to be a good thing.

'There were a lot more cattle here in the twenties and thirties, too. When I moved to Denton in 1942 there were twenty-two people working there; now there are three. Then I was at Street Farm, a name I always thought rather funny because there was very little in the way of a street running by the farm then. It had just forty acres, and we kept sixteen cows and a hundred pigs. I was married by this time, and when my son and daughter had grown up a bit they helped me. Farmers never took holidays in those days, they just couldn't, and it was a hard life by today's standards, I suppose. I took five weeks holiday in total in my ninety-two years.'

There was no bitterness or envy in Will's account of his early farming days; as he said himself, he grew up at a time when you accepted your lot, when Church and state and everything you knew or came across emphasised the impossibility of avoiding your fate. If your father was a land worker or a farmer, then ninety-nine times out of a hundred that's what you would be, and it was almost sinful to think of anything else. And a boy would learn the rudiments of agriculture as they had always been learned, not in any formalised way, but simply by watching and doing simple tasks until he was ready for more. It was a system honoured simply by long usage.

'Yes, I learned how to farm mostly by watching other people. When I was very young I remember my father gave an old farm-worker sixpence to look after me and show me what to do. But all my family had been farmers or farm-workers for centuries and I suppose I was born to it. It just seemed to come natural to me. My father managed four farms in all, and we lived at one of the four, Rose Farm where I was born. When the owner died he wanted Dad to take over Rose Farm, which reluctantly he did. My mother died in 1924, but death was an everyday occurrence then, with little medicine and few doctors and no science; I don't think the doctors knew much at all about anything much. When the man I worked for died in 1922 I went back to work for my father. Then I got a job as a cowman at Stanton, where I got a house with the job and had about twenty cows a day to milk. It all seems very small beer now, I know, but all the farms then, like the fields themselves, were small and a man made a living, not a fortune, on a farm.'

Once he was living in his own house, Will took stock

of his situation and resolved to raise enough money to rent his own farm, even though it was a rare thing in those days for a farm-worker to earn more than the absolute minimum necessary for survival. And even as he dreamed of his own farm, the long working days continued; his overriding memory of winter was always of ploughing and of the harshness of the weather.

Summer memories were very different.

'My strongest memory of summer is of milking the cows and the heat, the sweat in my eyes and the flies everywhere. And of course the cows in a mood and spinning about and kicking when you tried to milk them. I was the cowman at Denton for about three years, after which I seem to recall I was much in demand, for some reason. Whatever was behind it, there were plenty of farmers willing to offer me a job – they all seemed to want my services!'

Will laughed: 'I chose the farmer at a place called Dickleburgh, not so far from Scole, where the job was to manage about a hundred acres owned by a butcher. Part of my pay was the chance to work an allotment of land, free of rent. That was a real chance then, because in the thirties farming had no money in it at all, and if I'd had to pay anything to have that bit of an allotment there'd have been no point in taking it. I cleared it of weeds – it hadn't been touched in years – and I got a little money by cultivating it in my spare time. I used to work all day on the butcher's farm, and then pull up my own beets at night by hand; I'd be at it all night with often no sleep for a week. I was there from 1922 until 1942, when I was able to take Street Farm.

'I was always very much a one-man band, and a very

small farmer by today's standards, and, as I've said, I only ever had my son and daughter to help. My rent in my first year at Street Farm was £28 for the half year – farm rent was paid in April and October, at Lady Day and Michaelmas. I had nothing much at all when we moved to that farm, a few sticks of furniture, a bed and little else. But my wife was able, and soon got what little we had into manageable shape.'

Although it was clearly a hard life, Will at last had a place of his own, and there was just a little more time for the pleasures of life. 'When we were young and first married it wasn't all work, and although there was no television or radio and we never went anywhere, everyone else was in much the same boat – except the toffs, of course – so it didn't matter much. I remember we played dominoes and draughts as children, but none of the houses had much light then, or heating, just a big old fire and a few candles or oil lamps a bit later on, so it was cold and dark; but I don't remember being particularly uncomfortable, and you had to go to bed early anyway, to be up early to work.

'When I was a little older I used to go to Diss at weekends to whist drives and dances, so we had some fun. We did go to pubs, too, but I always remembered my father's warning that pubs were for man's use not for man's abuse. Pubs were dingy old places in those days, full of smoke and not a woman in sight; a woman wouldn't go near a pub then because if she did, it was automatically assumed that she was a prostitute. There were no exceptions to that.'

Undoubtedly the pub was an important place of relaxation for country people, and Will's recollection of the atmosphere of the pubs he knew was remarkably vivid: 'Every pub looked more or less the same when you went in: a big fire, a few scrubbed deal tables, dark low ceilings and a few old boys sitting round with their mugs of beer and smoking hard; everyone smoked short clay pipes for all they were worth. When you went in a pub you couldn't see through the smoke some days, and people nowadays think cigarettes are bad! Mind you, with a few candles or an oil lamp the only light, it wasn't surprising you could see so little. Besides, there was nothing much to see in most pubs since people went there to drink and play cards. Things were very different then – you went in the pub and the first thing the landlord does is give you a pipe! That's what used to happen when he knew you.

'My father hated a new pipe, so when the landlord gave him a new one he'd straightaway give it to another old boy till it had been smoked black, then my father would have it back. He liked 'em well worn in; he used to say it improved the flavour of the smoke.'

Many of the pub regulars were agricultural dealers, there to strike a bargain over a glass and a pipe, and this was particularly true on busy market days when many of the pubs did most of their trade. On other days the pub bar might remain empty for, as Will said, 'there were very few visitors, no tourists or holiday makers'; it was local men or nothing. On market day, however, the men would make a big thing of the pubs:

'They would go from pub to pub. I remember one old boy, Tom Reeve, who would have been fifty or sixty when I was a boy. He used to drink in the King's Head in Scole after tying his pony and cart up outside. Well, one day it ran off and we all watched him tearing down the road after it. We had a good laugh over that!' Such small misfortunes could be a source of amusement; but eager to dispel the myth of a rural golden age, Will also remembered how quick men were to argue and even to fight with bare knuckles.

'People were a lot rougher then than they are now, and in pubs there were always fights, and on the least provocation. A man might knock you down just because you looked at him for a second or two too long, and the worst offence was to pick up another man's beer – if you did, there was a very good chance he'd knock you down for it without a word.

'We're all a lot better behaved towards each other now, whatever the papers say. In those days some men went round deliberately looking for a fight; it was their bit of excitement, I suppose, even though they sometimes came off worse for the encounter.

'I remember once when I was a mere boy I was keeping score at dominoes for a couple of old boys in the pub. Well, I made a mistake and pegged the board wrong for one of them, and in a second he jumped up as if to hit me. But I was lucky because the landlord stopped him – and I was a just a boy, remember. I don't know why we were all like that then, but it was a common thing to fight, and the fights could be nasty.

'Perhaps it was the fact that communities were very isolated. I hardly knew anyone who'd been more than a couple of dozen miles from our area, and no one had been to London or could tell me anything about it. The roads were narrow and overgrown in most places outside the villages and they were covered with rough stones, not tar as they are now. Yes, I think it was the isolation, and the idea that a man was only worth anything if he was good with his fists – we couldn't feel good about out jobs or our cars because the former were all the same, and we didn't have any cars. Never seen 'em!'

With no responsibility for the roads beyond the parish boundary, road repair was a local matter carried out haphazardly, if at all; and that meant villages could be cut off not just by snow, but also by heavy rain, which might make the smaller roads impassable for days. 'Old women were paid to pick stones from the field into heaps, and these were used on the roads,' remembered Will. 'The women got two bob a ton, I think. They had to put them in heaps and then the farmer would collect all the stones in a cart and carry them to the road where a lot of very old men, perhaps from the workhouse, were employed to break the stones into small pieces and spread them on the road. Keeping the roads in a half decent state was almost a year- round job, because by winter there were always new potholes to fill and if they weren't filled quickly they got deeper and deeper.

'I think tar started to come in in the late 1920s, but then only for the main roads. The tar was heated up in a big iron pot pulled by horses; it was tipped onto the road and then levelled and swept back and forth by men with special brooms.'

The countryside may have been a busier place during the early years of the twentieth century, with most farms having numerous employees, but movement of goods, animals and men was expensive and it was therefore kept to a minimum. Moreover the idea of travel for the pleasure of travel itself was quite unheard of in poorer rural communities: 'Even horse traffic was scarce in the twenties and thirties; you could drive a cart for miles and you'd rarely pass another. Most people walked everywhere – my mum and dad didn't even have a bicycle, and only people with a fair bit of money could afford a pony and a trap. They might have a horse and cart for moving things around the place, but that was about it; my dad in his whole life never even went as far as Norwich.

'I would occasionally get a lift on the dickie seat at the back of a carriage, but they only took me along so that I could hop out whenever we reached a gate that had to be opened; but that was my travel and I enjoyed it. There were different horses kept for the different forms of transport: hackneys were for riding and showing, ponies pulled traps and small carts and, of course, there were ordinary carthorses for the heavy waggons.

'For my first few jobs as a lad I was sent all over the place to do all sorts of different jobs – I went feeding bullocks for a while, and was then sent to a shepherd at lambing time. I remember the weather was terrible, so we used what we called "lamb clothes", round hurdles designed to keep the wind off the lambs in their first few vulnerable hours. The shepherd had a tiny hut out in the fields about twelve feet square, with a wooden bench at one side and a stove that he kept burning continually with wood, and a chair where I sat, while the candle threatened to go out at any moment in the draught. The shepherd lay on the hard bench. He lived there all the time the sheep were lambing and could never wash or anything; but in those days no one worried very much about that anyway since no one had a bath in their house or even an inside loo – just a hole dug in the garden. When it filled up you dug another. Someone in his family brought the shepherd food every day, and when lambing was over he left the hut for another year.

'We always had big fires at home when I was a boy, one in the kitchen and one in the living-room. Mother baked once a week on a Friday and washed on a Monday; that was the way a woman was expected to do it, and if she didn't she was considered beyond the pale. I suppose in every area of life there was a way to do things and it was strictly adhered to. Any deviation was frowned on.'

The Great War did much to weaken the old ways and the often repressive unwritten rules that governed everyday life in the English countryside, but the hard facts of life in isolated rural communities were unavoidable, and nowhere more so than in the field of medicine.

'I had four brothers and three sisters who all died in infancy,' remembered Will, 'and most families had lost little children – disease was everywhere, particularly TB and smallpox, and of course if you had no money you couldn't get a doctor even if you were dying. My father ran four miles for the doctor soon after one sister was born, and the doctor brought my father back with him in the pony cart; I remember that as if it was yesterday, though it must be nearly eighty years ago. The vet was another character who'd give you a lift if you went to get him – but he'd only do it if it was wet and you agreed to catch his pony for him first!'

Though horses are a common sight today, it is difficult to imagine just how they dominated life in town and country before the coming of the motor car. According to Will they were the backbone of all work, but they were also intimately connected with the division between the social classes.

'I remember the pub stables – every pub stables – were always lined with horses, or they'd be tied up in the street at rings fixed in the brickwork of the wall. No one we knew rode a horse around the place; that was something only the toffs could afford because you needed a saddle, bridle and a proper riding horse to do it – a hackney would cost a great deal more than a pony or a carthorse. Besides, if you'd tried it people would've thought you'd gone mad, aping the gentry, and they wouldn't have taken too kindly to it. It just wasn't for the likes of us so we didn't aspire to it.'

Agricultural wages in the 1920s and 1930s were very

low: Will's first wages as a man were nine shillings a week, and a married man got ten shillings. Men like Will's father couldn't read or write although some might manage their own name; but he and Will were luckier than many because Will's mother *could* write, so she kept the farm books and entered the figures in a great ledger.

'Beer cost tuppence a pint just after the Great War, but it was very hard to live. And the workhouses were always full; if you didn't or couldn't work, that's where you might well end up,' remembered Will. So like his fellows, Will worked most days from dawn until dusk.

'On my first farm we ploughed all but a few of the one hundred acres, all but a meadow of about six acres. We'd plough from late September until January, and when the horses weren't ploughing we'd use them to cart things. Our barley we used to sell to the maltsters for beer – we had to take it to Diss or Eye in what were known as cwmb sacks. Our cart would hold thirty sacks of wheat or barley, and thirty sacks made roughly three tons, which it took three horses to pull. We'd travel with a load like this at about three miles an hour because we'd never trot the horses, always walk them. You'd get the sack for trotting them – that was a certainty if you were found out. Trotting was bad for their legs.

'It's easy enough to drive a great heavy waggon and three horses so long as you let the horses get on with it. I used to sit on the front of the beet waggon with the reins tied loosely on the harness: driving by mouth, we called it; in other words I'd just tell the horses what to do, and I never had to use the stick or the reins. When ploughing I used to show off by doing it with no line – with no reins, that is, and again by word of mouth. The old men didn't like it and said the horses would run away one day, but they never did. To get them to turn left we'd shout "Cum 'ere", and for right "Whisht".

'We used to go about on Saturdays to the drawing matches, and I won a lot of prizes at this. The prizes were usually given by local tradespeople and the first prize was nearly always a copper kettle; other prizes would be tools of one sort or another. On a Saturday we might walk as far as Wortham, eight miles away. At a drawing match the horses and ploughs were already there, and you'd just draw one furrow. For ploughing matches you had to plough with your own team and you had to do a certain minimum number of furrows, perhaps twelve or twenty. It was all judged on how level your ploughing was. Bad ploughing is very easy to spot, but there wasn't much of that where we were because the ploughmen who entered the matches really knew their stuff.

'In the last days of horse-ploughing men would drive round in cars to take part in the different matches – like that they could clean up on the prizes; and then suddenly it was all over for ever and the horses had gone.'

Away from the ploughing matches the great passion of the men was a pub game called quoits, and at one time almost every pub in Norfolk resounded to the clang of the quoits

irons. Now the game has vanished almost as completely as the horse-ploughing matches. 'Quoits matches were always being played in every pub yard. A quoit is a ring of iron weighing as much as eleven pounds. There was an iron peg with a feather stuck in it that was driven into the centre of what we used to call the quoit bed, a clay area designed to make the quoits slow down or stick a bit. No money was ever bet, but a gallon or two of beer might go to the winner of a game and the loser then bought the beer. You had to throw your quoits eighteen yards and each man had two quoits. Four men would play at any one tie. The last place I saw it played was at Billingford Common in the 1950s. Like horses, it just seemed to reach the end of its days and it disappeared, but the men loved it all over Norfolk. I suppose the men who played it had done so since they were young and still enjoyed it, but by the time they passed away their sons had other interests, motorbikes and cars.'

As he neared the end of his life, Will's views were still based on an intensely practical vision of the world, a belief in the need simply to get on with living; but even in the narrow isolated environment of 1920s rural Norfolk he was also aware of other, very different lives. 'The local toff round Scole was Sir Edward Mann; he owned all the land round about and all the farmers were his tenants. I can't say he was a bad landlord, although I know many others were, but we only saw him and his family when they were pheasant shooting and we'd perhaps beat for them. They lived what seemed to us a completely cut-off sort of a life, though we never questioned it. Sir Edward's grandson is at Billingford Hall now, so it goes on. They never met their tenants because it was all done through an agent.

'I think old people had the worst of it when I was a young man. I've lived into the age of social security, but back then, if they had no one to look after them they starved or froze to death. Neighbours might help, but a man could easily end in the workhouse and many would rather die in a ditch than that. It wasn't easy for women, either, particularly if they had husbands who spent all their wages in the pub. And many did, while their wives struggled to bring up twelve or thirteen children in a tiny cottage without heat or light or water as they are known today.

'Everything was different then, every detail. If you could go back in time the first thing you would notice is that everyone wore drab clothes, black or brown or some other nondescript colour. All the women wore ankle-length dresses when I was a boy, and leather, button-up boots. The men always wore hob-nailed boots made of the thickest leather, and if they got soaked they'd be as hard as hell the next morning when you came to put them on; and tough though they were, they would generally last only a year. But we wore them every day and a man only ever had the one pair. A pair of boots might cost fifteen shillings, and I reckon every working man in Norfolk wore the same sort. It wasn't until the 1930s that I got something different: lace-up rubber boots, which lasted as long as leather boots but were more comfortable. We all wore waistcoats, too – the men I mean – and special ploughman's trousers of soft thick cloth.

'My strongest memories are of the terrible struggle I had to scrape enough money together to take my own farm; I only managed it at last because I had that old allotment land rent free. I used to borrow a plough and a horse to work it, but as you know, I had no time during the day because I was working for another man. So I worked all day and then all night, without a bit of sleep. When I did rent a farm I was afraid of failing at it, but I knew I had to try, and that I would work from light till dark to make a go of it. Many days I carried 120 bags one after another from the thresher to the cart, and that was a hard business because a sack might weigh two or three hundredweight.'

Will's memories stretched back beyond even the steam traction engines and binders that began to infiltrate Norfolk in the 1920s and 1930s, and his descriptions of some aspects of farm life had an almost eighteenth-century ring to them. 'Barley and hay and corn were all cut by hand when I first started, all done with scythes as it had been from time immemorial. The way it was done meant that the men in a field couldn't all start at once. We were very systematic about it. The headman would start mowing up the field first and one by one the others would fall in behind and to the right-hand side of him. Perhaps fifteen men would mow, and if the weather was right it would all be carted loose. There would be two on top of the cart and two on the ground forking the hay up to them. The men on the cart laid the hay carefully in a circle because if you put it on the cart any old way you wouldn't get much on. Four of us might cart ten acres in a day in this way, and we'd take it in to the farmyard and unload it.

'Our ricks were normally ten yards by five yards, roughly the height of a twenty-stave ladder, and they would have thatched roofs just like a house. To thatch the roof you'd make up what we called a yelum [yealm: meaning bundle] of straw; you'd put six yelums in a yoke [wooden fork or hod] and then tie that with rope; up on the stack a man would undo the yoke and pin it to the stack with an iron clip. Bit by bit the whole thing would be pinned and covered, nice and waterproof.

'All our milk went to Diss and from there on the train to London; we took it to the station every day, and twice a day in summertime. When we were taking cattle to market we'd drive them into Diss; in those days there were gates everywhere along the roads so the cattle couldn't wander off into people's gardens or into fields. Pigs were driven along the road just the same and we never lost any, even when we walked them to Norwich, as occasionally we did.

'I didn't really retire till I was eighty-three, and I was married for sixty-five years; and in all that time I've never been further than Denton, about twelve miles away. Never been abroad or to London, and never wanted to, really. Always plenty of pubs enough in this area! Farming's a lot easier now; the fields are bigger for the machinery, and the animals have mostly gone and the farm-workers: my son makes a better living than I did as a young man – and good luck to him!'

HIGH DAYS
& HOLIDAYS

REG DOBSON

NEWTON, WARWICKSHIRE

*A*mid the crowded towns and cities of the English Midlands there are occasional green oases, and tucked away in one of these and just a few miles from the busy town of Rugby is Reg Dobson's Home Farm. It has changed little since it was built three hundred or more years ago and it has a curious feel to it, with staircases hidden behind doorways and bedrooms tucked away in odd corners here and there, and in under the eaves.

Reg who died in his late eighties, helped his son to run their farm long after he had officially retired; and like so many traditional farmers he looked back with great fondness to the days when farming was a way of life rather than a means simply to make money. Even towards the end of his long life, Reg had an unusually vivid memory for the mass of incident and detail from long ago, and he was a fund of marvellous stories about the characters he knew as a boy and as a young man. Though he had farmed in Warwickshire since the 1950s he started life on a farm further west in deepest Shropshire, as he explained when I met him in the 1990s in his massive kitchen with its beamed ceiling and roaring fire.

'I was brought up at a place called Cheswardine Park at Market Drayton; I had one brother and four sisters, and I was the eldest. We had a big old house, and it always seemed to be crowded with people; I think all farmhouses were well filled in those days because so many people worked on the land, and by tradition they lived in with the farmer and his family. So as well as us children and my parents we had a nursemaid, a kitchenmaid, my aunt Katy and her son George.

'My mother was a very kindly woman, and although she died when I was only nine I remember her well. One thing that was particularly unusual about her was that she would not tolerate any cruelty to the farm animals – that may not sound so special now, but in those days people cared a lot less about animal welfare.

'On Saturday nights we were always bathed in a tin bath in front of a massive log fire. I remember I once refused to get undressed, so the nursemaid undressed me; but when she turned her back I bolted through the back door and out into the pitch-dark garden – after a long chase I was caught, however, and carried back to the house.

Reg took great delight in talking about the past, and he had a genuine ability to bring it alive: 'I can't remember ever really falling out with my brothers and sisters, though I do remember once making my sister eat coal, which we used to feed to the pigs for the minerals! We used to walk across the fields to school unless it was very wet, and then mother or one of the girls in the house took us in the pony and trap. We loved that.

'Horses were a big part of my life because Dad had made a lot of money during the Great War by selling horses. We were quite well dressed and shod, unlike a lot of children and adults at that time. Mother used to give the poor our old clothes and shoes. We had hens, and in those days of course every hen in the country was free range – they just wandered about the yard and we fed them on wheat and maize. However, the grain used to attract hundreds of sparrows and this annoyed us, so we used to catch them by tying a long piece of string to a coal riddle and propping it up on a stick. We'd then put a pile of corn under the riddle and when a sparrow landed we'd pull the string, down would come the riddle and we'd catch it! We used to give them to Mother who made them into pies. 'We were terrible then for using catapults – all country boys were – and we'd fire at anything and everything, I'm afraid. Mostly, though, we'd fire at empty glass bottles; in those days they used to have a marble inside, so when we'd broken the bottle with the catapult we'd collect the marbles. We became experts at marbles, my brother and I.

'After my mother died Father was away virtually all the time dealing in horses, land or one thing and another. 'One of my best childhood memories was of visits to my maternal grandparents. Grandma always made a big fuss of me, and for some reason she always insisted on buying my boots for me, I think perhaps because she'd worn shoes that were too tight when she was a girl. As a result she had to have a toe amputated when she was eighty – and without anaesthetic! I remember she just lay there and I held her hand while they cut off her toe: she never made a sound.

'Just before she died she lay in bed and pointed to a drawer in an old cupboard and said to me, "When I die, all the money in that drawer is for you." Alas, I never got a penny of it, because as soon as she died the housekeeper rifled the drawer and disappeared for ever with all the money!'

Reg's family had been farmers on both his mother's and his father's side for generations. His maternal grandfather was also a trained blacksmith and shod all his own horses on the farm. He had a great fondness for beer, too; every Wednesday he'd set off for Market Drayton, as

Reg recalls:

'He'd always take the horse and waggon – or float as we used to call it – and he'd invariably take his neighbour, who was an old friend, with him. They'd put the horse up at the pub – every pub had stables then – and proceed to get gloriously drunk. At chucking out time the publican would help them out of the door and into the waggon, then he'd lead the horse into the middle of the street and away they would go. They would soon fall fast asleep and the horse would slowly make his way home five miles away; he would walk into the yard where he would stop, then my grandma would come out to wake the two men up and give them a good telling-off, The telling-off never did any good, though, because the following week they'd be off again.'

Market Drayton seemed to be alive with characters like Uncle Arthur: 'He was one of the first in our area to get a car, though it was such an old banger that a horse had to pull it before it would start. He once drove all the way to Bishop's Castle on the wrong side of the road; if he met a waggon or another car (very rare) he would simply curse and yell at the other driver as if it was his fault that we were on the wrong side of the road!'

But apart from odd moments of hilarity, life in Shropshire in the early part of this century tended to be hard and unremitting, and this produced a tough independence of character, typified by Reg's father. 'Dad was a very fierce man; he had only to look at us and say "That will do", and we were terrified into silence. He'd taken over Cheswardine Park from his mother when she died, leaving him ten young brothers and sisters to look after. At the time, Cheswardine was in a very poor state, as were most farms in the twenties; but when he sold it years later it was one of the best farms in Shropshire. He was a tough, determined man.'

Inevitably horses were an important part of young Reg's life, and he always retained a keen interest in horse racing; for his father, however, horses were everything. 'He was horse mad: he just loved them, whether riding, driving or buying and selling them. I remember he bought two really good ponies for me – they were a bit wild, but that's what people wanted in those days; they only wanted quiet ones for the trap or cart, but lively ones to carry them around the place.

'I remember one filly we had which was kept in a loose box between two cowsheds; every night and morning we gave her about a gallon of milk straight from the cow. At about eighteen months Father took her to a racing trainer because she was such a likely looking horse; three months later she was dead from TB. She was rotten with it through and through. TB was rife in those days; we always lost two or three cows each year from TB, but people just accepted that it was a part of life then. It was called John's disease. Why we didn't get it I'll never know, particularly as my

father would never get rid of a sick cow – he'd always assume it would get better if you left it long enough.

'Dad was into livestock of all kinds. He used to breed greyhounds now and then, for example, and one of them won several races so my father sold it for a good price; it never won again! Animals were right at the heart of our lives, and we associated them with work as well as with good fun. For instance when we were very young we used to love to ride in the heavy carts when the men were bringing in the roots or mangels – though farms could be just as dangerous then as they are now; my sister fell out of a cart once and the great heavy wheel ran over her hand and completely crushed it. And then Father had a hell of a game getting the teachers at the school to let Dorothy learn to write with her left hand – in those days you had to write with your right hand even if it didn't work!' Soon it was time for Reg to go to boarding school, which he hated. 'I went from the village school to Adams Grammar School in Newport. The masters were very strict, and I was caned regularly; one master, Tubby Gill, used to beat us till we couldn't sit down! I left after four years, which was the best thing that ever happened to me. I was sixteen and started work full-time on the farm, which I loved.'

Escape from school might seem every schoolboy's dream come true, but for Reg it meant long hours and hard work – he was expected to work seven days a week, from six in the morning till six at night. There were 125 cows to milk by hand every day: 'Unless you've actually done that yourself you can have no idea of the work involved' he says now. 'There were twelve of us did the milking, and we did it according to a number system so that each person had his or her fair share of difficult cows – you know, cows that held their milk up or that kicked like hell. If they thought they could get away with it, people would deliberately take a long time at an easy cow until they could see that another easy one was next in line to be milked. We used to put a special leather strap on the kickers to keep their legs still, though some started to kick before you even got near them.

'An old man called Punch used to carry off the pails of milk as they were filled. He wore a great wooden yoke, like you'd put on a pair of oxen, with a pail hung on each side.

'In my first year I had to do the sheep, too, mostly Cheviots, and the devil to catch because we had no proper pens. I used to get the dog to hold them in a corner of the field and then run in and catch the one I wanted. Half the time it was a question of run in and dive at a fleeing sheep, a bit like a rugby tackle. An old local poacher called Jim Came used to come at shearing time. I used to turn the handle of the wheel that drove the shears – we'd come on a bit from simple hand-shears – and he did the clipping. He was very good at it, but it was hard work for a sixteen-year-old turning that thing all day.

'If you had any hope of surviving on a Shropshire farm early this century you had to be a shrewd dealer. Selling your produce in the days before intervention buying by the EC was the severest test of a farmer's ability in the market place. Dad was a sharp one for selling sheep. He'd buy them and get us to trim them and clean them till they looked really smart and then he'd take them straight back to market and usually get a pound or two more for each one than he'd paid for them.'

Self-sufficiency was important at a time when many farms were part of isolated communities, and much of the 300 gallons of milk a day the Dobsons' cows produced went to make cheese. The cheese was made on site by a cheese maker who lived in with the family; nothing was ever wasted, and the large quantities of whey, a by-product of the cheese making process, were stored and then fed to the pigs: 'It was kept in a big brick tank and I used to take it by bucketful to feed the pigs. I had a yoke on my shoulders which made it a bit easier, but it was incredibly hard work, particularly on your legs. In those days we had what would now be considered very unbalanced rations for the animals – we'd prepare a great barrow full of maize-germ meal and tip it in the pigs' trough, and then we'd pour the whey on top; there was an awful lot got trodden in and slopped about. These days animal feeding is a very scientific business.

'Most of the feed we were able to buy came on the train to Drayton which was three miles away, and it was a full day's work to take a cart there to collect the feed and get it back to the farm.

'Father always used to buy the biggest pigs he could find; they'd weigh seven or eight stone when he brought them home, and then we'd feed them till they weighed seventeen or eighteen stone apiece. When we took them to market they were really big, in fact one was so fat that it dropped dead as it walked up the ramp into the cart! I went with Father once to Welshpool and he bought every single pig in the market. One lot in a pen had great long snouts and I didn't think they'd do any good. "They're the best of the bunch," he said, and he was right.'

The pig was the great saving of many farmers and smallholders. It was a hardy animal that grew quickly and could be relied on to hoover up every kind of vegetable waste and turn it into delicious bacon.

'We loved it when we killed a pig,' remembers Reg, 'which may sound terrible, but you have to remember that a lot of people went hungry in those days and there was no time for sentimentality. When we killed a pig we ate every last bit of it. We had the liver and kidneys, and sausages and pork pies were made from some bits, pork scratchings from the skin. We even used the bladder, as with a bit of effort you could turn it into a really good football. You just blew it up and tied a knot in it and it lasted for ages!'

Reg Dobson has a positive, no-nonsense outlook, and is dismissive of what he sees as fads and fancies among townsfolk. 'Today, all the talk is about animal fat killing you. Well, let me tell you, we lived on it. For breakfast we'd have two eggs, six rashers of fat bacon and fried bread with masses of dripping, and this would be after porridge with huge dollops of cream all over it. Mind you, we had to work like blazes so I suppose we worked it off; and we've all lived to a pretty ripe old age, too, except my brother Lionel who was only forty-three when he died.'

Standards of hygiene on those Shropshire farms would shock many people today, but with water available only from a well, and no mains gas or electricity, a big family had to take a far more practical view of these matters. 'After a day's work in the farmyard we'd be covered in muck of one sort or another, but we only rarely had a change of trousers. Trousers were just trousers and we wore them all the time whatever their state – and there were no wellies or overalls. When you came in you just sat by the fire and the muck dried on you and steamed away. No one thought anything of it, it was just the way things were.'

There is no doubt, too, that you had to be very ill

indeed to be excused a day's work, even if you were the farmer's son. 'I had serious problems with my left hip when I was a young man; it was displaced, and eventually the doctor told my father I should not carry anything heavy – but I still had to work, and had to help old Jack with the cows. Jack was an old soldier who had a bad right leg, and I often thought we must have looked a lovely couple walking across the farmyard, him limping one way and me the other!'

A typical day for Reg would start at 5.30am: he would put hay in the racks at the head of each cow's stall, and then the milking would begin, and 'No one under the age of sixty or seventy will remember what it was like to feed and muck out 125 cows every day,' he says with a wry smile. Women and men would start work together in the mornings; after breakfast they would let the cattle out to water, as none was piped to the farm in those days, and then roots and mangolds would be mixed together with corn and mash as feed.

'There was no cattle cake in those days, I'm afraid,' says Reg. 'Then we'd muck out. That was a perilous job, I can tell you, because we always seemed to have so little straw and the muck was almost liquid. We used to load it into a barrow and then push the barrow on to the top of the midden, where we tipped it. After a few years the midden might be twelve feet high, and at that height with a slippery muck-covered plank there were bound to be accidents. I've slipped off that plank many times and ended up waist-deep in cow muck!'

'After cleaning out, we fed the cows individually, and you had to be smart while you were at it or the greedy ones ate up first and then started knocking the others around. There was also the risk of being kicked; if you were, in those days you'd belt the cow with a stick or with the milking stool, though eventually I realised that this made them worse, and that if you were kind and gentle they responded in the same way. Nowadays we never put a stick on our animals.'

Reg's memories of Cheswardine Park are characterised by his sense of camaraderie and good fun, the spirit of enjoyment that seems to have survived in spite of the long hours of hard work in all weathers. Many of the men and women Reg worked with became friends for life, and one or two, like Reg Boffey, married into the family.

'Reg eventually married one of my sisters; he used to cut the hay while I forked it in to the animals, and we had great fun together, but he was a devil for cutting the wads bigger and bigger. They'd start at about a yard square and soon be two yards square, and the more he could get on the pikel the better he liked it. One day I just managed to stagger out of the barn with a massive load he'd put on my fork, then collapsed in the yard with all the hay on top of me. I didn't think much of it, but he fell about laughing.

'We were always playing good-natured jokes on each other and on the others. I remember Frank Chidlow who used to cart for us – we used to fill his cart so full of muck at muck-spreading time that his horse couldn't budge it an inch. We thought it was hilarious, even though we straightaway had to lessen the load to get the thing moving; either that or Frank would go and get what we called a chainhorse to help pull the cart. And he'd cuss his head off at us while he did it.

'When he was courting a girl at Northwich Reg used to get back to the farm in the early hours, and he'd shake me and say "Sam, it's time to get up!" I'd leap out of bed in a panic, and he'd immediately jump into the warm place I'd made in the bed. We were both called Reg, but for some reason we called each other "Sam" all the time, Lord knows why. We used to share the same bed, and the room had two windows which we kept open winter and summer however hard the weather. Some mornings the jerry would be frozen over it got so cold.'

Like many rural areas, Shropshire had its fair share of eccentrics, frequently elderly, often highly superstitious men and women who had spent their lives in tiny out-of-the-way cottages, eking out a living by occasional or seasonal farm-work. 'Pay was very low in the twenties and thirties. A man would get just a few shillings a week, his wife less, even if she came to milk night and morning. Apart from Sunday, the farm-workers had only one day a year off Good Friday, but even then they had to come and milk. However, they'd get a cottage with a big garden so they grew all the vegetables they needed, and they usually kept a pig – and that was all the meat a poor man ever got, except for rabbits.

'Frank Chidlow, our waggoner, had eight children and little money, so when he wanted a beer he'd catch himself a dozen or more rabbits and exchange them for a few pints at the local pub. When he'd had a few pints he'd start to sing, which the other regulars loved, so they'd start buying him more drinks. He'd get back to the farm at three in the afternoon, have his dinner and then go to milk; half-an-hour later he'd be fast asleep on the milking stool. Frank's wife, Olive, used to milk, too; when she was pregnant she'd milk until the day before she went into labour, and she'd be back at work the day after the child was born.'

The pub was very much the centre of social life in Reg's youth, and men would walk out miles every evening to drink at their favourite local – which might be five or six miles away if they lived in one of the many remote cottages. The pub gave men their only chance to escape the drudgery of everyday life; for the price of a few pints they could enjoy a temporary escape into a world of laughter and good fellowship.

Another pastime Reg recalls was the tug-o-war: 'We used to have horseback tug-o-wars with teams from the various farms and big houses competing. We had one once at the big house where Colonel Donaldson Hudson lived, the local squire; he entered a team, as did the surrounding farms, and we got to the final where we had to pull against the Colonel's team.

'As we got going and took up the strain, one of our horses started misbehaving; so Father put his coat over her head to calm her, but that made her worse and she reared. Bubber, a wild old boy and a great giant of a man, slipped off her – everyone was riding bareback – but we still held our own. Then seizing his chance, Bubber leapt back on, gave an almighty heave and all the Colonel's men and horses were pulled over. So we'd won; but we were disqualified because you had to let the Colonel's team win. That was the way they thought in those days.

'We used to get our own back on him, though, by laying trails of raisins the day before he was to have a big shoot; the raisins, which pheasants love, led to our wood and of course as a result we had plenty of pheasants!

'Eating competitions were a big thing in my youth in Shropshire, and I believe this was true of many other country districts; I suppose it was good, simple entertainment when we had little else. The waggoner on a farm near us was a phenomenal eater, and people used to come and fetch him to eat for bets. One night a farmer knocked at his door and asked his wife if he would come and eat a whole calf for a bet. She wasn't in the least surprised by the request, but didn't know if he would because he'd already gone out to eat two ducks down at the Fox for a bet. "I'll go down there and ask him," said the man. He found Bill, put the proposition to him and Bill, having eaten his ducks, went off straight away and ate the calf as well!'

Food was thus a source of great entertainment as well as being one of life's great pleasures, although one or two food sources – most notably rabbit – were not highly thought of at all; perhaps because there were so many of them and they were considered the staple of the very poorest, few liked the idea of dining regularly on rabbits. But if you found yourself in a tight corner financially you could always catch enough rabbits to earn a few bob: 'It was no trouble in those days to catch a hundred rabbits in a day – they were everywhere, and I think most of the men on the farm virtually lived on rabbit. A great friend of mine called Cyril used to be mad about cricket, just as I was, and once we went and caught rabbits and sold them until we had enough money to get to Old Trafford on the train to watch England play the Australians.'

Killing rabbits and pigs, and twisting the necks of chickens for the pot, were all part of the less-than-idyllic farming scene which held sway earlier this century; and 'closeness to nature' probably contributed to what Reg still describes as 'a kind of roughness of character. There's no doubt we were a rough bunch in some ways: I remember one girl used to tease Cyril and me, so we picked her up and dropped her in a barrel of treacle – well, you've never seen such a sight in your life, she could hardly walk; but she never teased us again.

'We were positively medieval in our attitudes to hygiene in those days, too. I don't think it was so much that we didn't care, it was just that without running water, plastic overalls and all the other modem hygiene aids, you just had to accept that things were going to be done as they'd always been done. For example, I've explained how the cows were let out into the fields to water before we had water piped to the sheds. Well, as they went out through the narrow gateways where all the muck and slurry would accumulate, inevitably they got into a terrible mess. But we used to wipe their udders with just an old piece of sacking, and you can imagine what the milk was like after that! When we stopped making cheese on the farm we started to sell the milk to the chocolate company Nestle, and the colour of the milk was like chocolate when we sent it to them! They were always writing to Father to complain, sowe started washing the cows properly; but I don't think it really made a lot of difference.

'We were only in this position because we didn't have all the modem conveniences. Take haymaking, for example: younger people on farms today have no idea what a hard job haymaking used to be. Frank Chidlow would go out with the horses at 3am because he needed to work virtually twenty-four hours a day to get the job done in time; and of course in summer it was cooler working at that time in the morning. Actually Frank loved the horses and he'd often arrive earlier than he needed just to groom them all properly.

'When I moved here in the fifties, Frank came and sowed a field of oats for me. It ran by Wattling Street, and he put a stick at either end to get a straight line and made a hell of a fuss before starting because, as he said, "I'm not having anybody go up the Wattling and say, what a mess that field is!', At a time when ordinary men and women had few possessions of any note, their greatest pride lay in their work and in what other people thought of their efforts. As Reg observed: 'Oh, yes, when I was young all the men would walk all round the different farms on a Sunday, and if any field had been badly ploughed or sown it would be all over the village in no time. Today no one minds what a field looks like, so long as it is all done quickly.'

It is difficult nowadays to conceive the level of poverty at which most agricultural workers once lived. Reg describes how Frank Chidlow and his wife and eight children all survived on £2 a week in a tiny cottage. 'How he did it I'll never know, but they all grew up strong and well,' he says.

If the men were indomitable, with rich, idiosyncratic characters, the same was certainly true of many of the farm animals: 'They were real characters. I remember one of our cows had a massive udder, or bag as we used to call it; we used to have to get two people to milk her, one on each side. She was a gentle thing, though; once when we had four orphaned lambs we put two on each side of this massive udder and she stood quite still and let them feed.

She reared them, too, and they used to follow her about everywhere when we turned them out into the spinney.'

The labour-intensive nature of milking and of dealing with pigs and other farm animals was matched by the almost complete absence of technology on the arable fields. 'For our one hundred acres of hay, all we had in the way of implements was a turner, a device drawn by a horse that flipped the hay over so that it would dry evenly, and an old horse-rake. After the hay had been dragged up into piles we'd cock it up by hand into small heaps to keep the rain off as much as possible. Next day, or soon after, it had all to be shaken out and turned again by hand. When it was ready to cart, we pitched it onto the waggon by hand, one man on top, one each side of the waggon. Then we had to rope it on because the old cart-tracks were a bit rough and the bumps as we went along might otherwise have thrown the whole lot off. Back in the yard we pitched it into the hayloft by hand, and we'd often be at it until midnight or beyond.

'All the men were real artists when it came to hay, and hated slap-happy methods. Haymaking used to last from about mid-June to about the end of August.'

Rain was an obvious problem at haymaking time, but too much sun could also make it difficult, as Reg recalls: 'I remember Frank Chidlow cut me a fourteen-acre field of hay one year, and it was so hot that before I could get it in cocks it was already over-made – that is, too dry. We started to cart it in the horse waggon, but we had a heck of a game because it was so brittle – it started to fall off every time we had half a load on, and I don't think there was much goodness left in it anyway.

'Another time we were in the local pub one Sunday

and we decided that after our dinner we would carry Harry Robinson's field – all the men helped each other at harvest time. Anyway, the pub was full, and after we'd had our fill we all trooped out and set to, eleven of us with the horses and waggons. I helped build the rick with the others pelting the sheaves up to us at a terrific rate. We did it very fast, but what a mess we had at the end of it! The rick was leaning towards the road at an angle of about 45 degrees and we had to get every pole from a radius of about a mile to prop it up! It was such a sight that someone sketched it and hung the picture in the pub that night!'

Cheswardine Park was a long way from the nearest town and with four girls and three young men living in close proximity, relationships were bound to develop, and pregnancy and scandal were never far away. 'If a girl got pregnant in those days it was a terrible disgrace. I had to pay five shillings a week for eighteen years to one young girl I made pregnant. She had the child and I paid the money, but I've never seen either of them since. I was only a lad at the time. I remember, too, that three of our bailiffs married three of our cheese makers and Dad helped set them up on farms of their own. He was always doing that sort of thing. He lent them £250 apiece, but only one ever paid him back: he sent Father £500 about twenty years after marrying and taking his loan – Dad was highly delighted.

'Another great character was Tom Bennett, the champion hedge-layer of the whole of Shropshire. If he didn't get first prize for the best hedge-laying one year he'd get it for the best grown hedge the next. Every job he did was perfect. He used to cut our lawn with a scythe as good as any modem lawn-mower could do it. He was a great rick-builder, too, and when he'd finished he'd often come back at night to pull out the loose bits of hay just to make sure it looked perfect.

'Tom used to chew tobacco twist and he was a deadly accurate spitter – he once hit a cat on the head at about twenty feet! And he had amazing teeth; he used to bite into an iron railing at the bottom of the garden and swing from it. Tom never went anywhere in his whole life, to the best of my knowledge, except one trip after he retired when he got the bus to the Royal Show at Lincoln; but he got lost, missed the bus back, and spent £20 – a small fortune – on a taxi to get home. That was the first and last time he went anywhere!'

One theme that runs throughout Reg's endless series of delightful anecdotes is that in country districts in days gone by, people almost invariably made their own entertainment, and often this meant playing jokes on each other, which was all usually taken in good part. 'I remember two fat butchers used to call at Charlie Denton's place in a pony and trap. They were so fat that when they got in the trap the horse was nearly lifted up in the air. One day Charlie's boys undid the horse's belly strap and as soon as the butchers got in the trap the shafts shot up in the air and they tumbled out into the road. We roared with laughter, but the air was blue with the butchers' curses.

'But country people could be very stick-in-the-mud, too. I remember we had a parish meeting when the council said they would pipe water to the village houses. The older inhabitants didn't want it because they said you could smell the ducks from Stamford Park when you turned the taps on (Stamford Park was the municipal lake where the water would come from). But in spite of all, the water came in the end, and so did electricity.

'After my mother died aunt Katy looked after us. She was lovely, and I think she loved my father but he loved somebody else – the local publican's daughter. She got divorced so she could marry Dad, which cost Dad £3,000, an absolute fortune in those days. After they were married they took a hotel in Liverpool for a while, but Dad hated it. In those days you had to be whiter than white to get a publican's licence, and because my stepmother was a divorcee she couldn't get the licence; it had to be in someone else's name. But by 1931 Dad was back on a farm; he just wasn't suited to city life.'

'A chap called Walter Thomas used to work for us and

he was a wonderful workman. He liked piecework, and he and his wife used to dig our potatoes. They'd dig eleven square roods a day, which is some going, and while they were doing it they used to camp in the field. Walter also used to pull our swedes, and he was so fast there'd be one landing on the heap, one flying through the air and one in his hand. He'd go on like that all day, and when we were all hoeing together he'd leave us standing if he felt like it.

'In winter he cut our hedges. He used a short-handled slasher, and as he was six feet tall and our hedges were rather small he could cut both sides as he went along simply by leaning over. As he cut, so his wife gathered the brashings and piled them up and burned them. They were a great team, but all they got for the work was 3d a rood. By working all the hours God sends – milking, hoeing, drilling, sowing and ploughing – they only made about £16 a week.'

It is important to remember that although Reg was officially the boss's son, there was no significant difference between his daily routine and that of the other farm-workers; they simply mucked in together. The only material difference was the fact that the farmer's son didn't get paid at all since his return would come in the long-term when he inherited the farm. This seems to have been pretty universal practice among all except gentlemen farmers with considerable sums of money.

Because he wasn't paid by his father, Reg had to find other ways to make money. 'I used to go long-netting for rabbits with Walter. One night we got fifty in one go. We also set traps, which I admit was very cruel and I'm glad it's stopped now. Country people did like eating rabbit, although if they had nothing else they got a bit tired of it.

We used to go to a local dance sometimes after rabbiting, but we smelled so strong of rabbits that none of the girls would dance with us. Never mind, we used to say, we can still get into the bar!'

Reg's tales of what was obviously a lively and generally happy farming community are not based on a rose-tinted view of the past. As well as the fun and the practical jokes, things could be difficult in a way that many of us find difficult to imagine today. 'In farming it certainly wasn't all good in the old days, and at times it was very difficult indeed to make ends meet. Before the Milk Marketing Board was set up, we had to take our milk to a cheese maker nearby and got 4½d per gallon for it; after the MMB that went up to 8½d. Selling privately and locally, as we had to do then, had some advantages but it would mean penury for the small farmer today.

'Farming was difficult and even dangerous in other ways, too – we often used to hear about people being fatally injured by their animals. It nearly happened to me once when we were leading a dangerous bull into a stall. Just as I reached down to put his chain on he whipped round and knocked me to the ground. He then knocked Jim, my stockman, over and started butting the stall. I was lucky and managed to crawl away, but either or both of us could easily have been killed.

'I met the girl I was eventually to marry when I was eleven, and even proposed to her one night; but then I went away to school and didn't see her again till I was nineteen. I used to cycle about eleven miles every night to see her, along rough roads and narrow, bumpy lanes. She learned to drive, although she never had any lessons; none of us did in those days. Her brothers taught her, just put her in the driving seat and showed her what to do.'

The church seems to have played a lesser part in the life of the countryside in the early part of this century than one might have imagined, but where it did have a strong influence, individual priests were often heartily disliked. Reg's memories of country parsons perhaps typify the two ends of the spectrum: the parson who was a friend of the community, and the one who let it be known that he felt he was far superior to his flock. 'I was very fond of one parson we had when we were in Shropshire. He used to play in the village cricket team in which I also played, and he said that there were only two things he was any good at: cricket and preaching. But another parson I remember was quite different, a real bad lot who treated all the children like dirt, and we hated him. He put me off parsons for life.'

The distinction between town and country was far less well defined in 1920s Shropshire than it is now. People who lived in towns were often only one generation away from a farming background, and as a result they tended to cultivate vegetables rather than just flowers in their gardens. Many kept chickens too, and even pigs. 'Lots of townspeople kept pigs then. There were no rules and regulations in the way there are now, and although they knew they'd eat the pig eventually they often treated it as a pet while it was with them. I remember some people we knew used to put their pig up on the garden wall so it could see the town band go past!

'But farming always came first in my family – I remember that when I eventually married Gladice we chose 10 September, and my father was most put out because it was also the date of the Ullesthorpe Sheep Fair and he had a hundred ewes to sell!

'When we were first married we lived in a way that you just can't imagine: we had a house with no electricity, no gas, no heating other than big old fires, no easy lighting, and no labour-saving devices at all. We had oil lamps for light, and everything had to be scrubbed clean without detergents and washing powers; it was all brute force and elbow grease, really. We had two children, both girls, and Gladice had read somewhere that fresh air was good for babies, so we'd leave them out for a couple of hours every day, even when a gale was blowing! But it didn't seem to do them any harm.

'Eventually we packed up the dairy herd, largely because I was fed up with milking and mucking out 365 days a year; though it's easier today with ready-made feeds. We then went in for suckler cows, fat cattle, sheep and about 140 acres of corn. Weeds were our biggest problem in the early days with corn because there were no chemicals, and although it looked pretty with millions of poppies it wasn't much good as a crop-when we harvested it the poppies made a hell of a stink. But all that is easier now with sprays and chemicals.

'But the minus side to all the modem innovations is that there are fewer people on the land, and a man is stuck in an air-conditioned tractor all day. A lot of the life and fun has gone out of it, and although I had a hard life it was fun and I enjoyed every minute of it.'

Fairy Tales

In rural Ireland, particularly the west of that country, it was usual well into this century to see the male children of small farmers dressed carefully as girls. The practice, which might last until a child was eight or ten, stemmed from a widely held belief that this was the only way to prevent their being stolen by the fairies.

Padraig O'Connor, *The Old Country*, 1937 *A Farm for a Fiddle*

Of all the seven liberal sciences that may best be spared, as least beneficial to a commonwealth and for my part I had rather (if you will believe me) that my feet should pace 1,000 acres of land of mine own, than my fingers to play 1,000 lessons on the best lute in town, though I might have it for my labour; and he that is not of my mind, it is pitie if he ever have 1,000 acres but he should change them for a fiddle.

George Arwell, *The Faithfull Surveyour*, 1663

Farming the Roman Way

Mr Tull's chapter on Virgilian husbandry is very curious. In it we clearly see that we have all our agricultural practices and notions from the Romans.

William Cobbett, *Introduction to the first posthumous edition of Jethro Tull's Horse-hoeing*, 1829

'The World's All Wrong'

JOE WHITE
CHAGFORD, DEVON

*O*n the edge of Dartmoor, just a few miles from the quiet market town of Chagford and hidden away in an all-too-easy-to-miss fold in the hills, lies Batworthy Farm. A long, gaunt-looking stone farmhouse, it is older than anyone seems able to guess; it was there when the Domesday Book was compiled, although even then it was almost certainly an ancient house. The lane that approaches the farm is probably as narrow and twisting, and assuredly just as deep as it was centuries ago, for Batworthy Farm has been all but left behind by the modern world. In the 1980s it was owned by Joe White. Joe had come to the farm as a child just after the end of the Great War ago and never left, sharing it in latter days with his sister Annie. The boundaries of his world were Chagford and Moretonhampstead, both just a few miles away, and of course the neighbouring farms, and in his long life Joe strayed outside Devon only once; he never went abroad, never learned to drive, and never took a holiday away from the farm.

His parents came to Barworthy from another long-hidden farm at Wiveliscombe in Somerset. Joe had no children of his own and was the last of generations of farmers; and he farmed with a deliberate and conscious purpose just as his ancestors did – his one concession to the twentieth century was an old tractor bought by his father in the 1960s. He always refused to use chemicals or nitrates on his land, maintaining that these 'make the grass grow too fast to be any good', and he only gave up using horses in the mid-1960s. He was one of the last farmers to give them up and it pained him greatly to do it: 'You can't beat a horse. A horse is a wonderful animal and don't let anyone tell you t'otherwise – even ploughing with a horse wasn't as hard as people make out. It's just quicker with a tractor, but why that's such a great thing I don't understand. It's all fast and faster today, but what this rushing is all for, I don't know. Everyone wants to do everything in a hurry. Why? What are they going to do with all the time they'll have left?'

The pace of Joe's life was assuredly in tune with the pace of the seasons and the land he farmed – a cliché often applied to rural lives, but never more justly used than in this instance. And horses matched that pace as the tractor and other modern contrivances never could; Joe's father always kept a good pony to ride into Chagford, and there were always at least three horses for ploughing and general use. And in the ancient stone barns dotted about Batworthy's one hundred acres were still the carts and ploughs, winnowing machines and mechanical potato pullers that Joe's father and grandfather used. When he was asked why he kept them, Joe would look at you as if you were mad because, as he used to say, 'no real farmer would get rid of 'em – I might use 'em again. Most of them still work and you never know, I might *have* to use them again!'

Joe's main barn was as big as the farmhouse itself, and it was situated just across the deep narrow lane that passed the farm; it had certain features which indicate that it may once have been used as a house long before the present house was built: gigantic beams held up the curved ceiling boards; the boards themselves were each two feet wide and each fit perfectly with its neighbour because they were cut one after another from the trunk of the same vast tree. Also, giant granite chimneys rose up at either end of the barn, their lintels made from massive, squared-off sections of oak. Neither house nor barn had mains electricity. 'We're not on the electricity here because they wanted twenty thousand pounds to put up ten poles to get it here!' said Joe, with a grin.

Another barn, made from equally huge blocks of roughly dressed stone, contained an ancient cider press and apple crusher. The great wooden wheel on the press with its enormous wooden teeth was all made by hand, each piece slotted into its rightful place with consummate skill by long-dead craftsmen. Even Joe had no idea how old the press was, but it was in use until the 1960s and Joe only gave it up because there were so few farmers and friends left with whom he could share the cider. 'All the farms, or most of 'em anyway, come up for sale when the old folks die, and they're bought by Londoners who come down and try to tell us how to do things. The children go away to college and don't come back, so the farms have all gradually been sold to strangers. It's a pity, but the world's all wrong and I suppose there's nothing we can do about it.'

In between regular and copious bouts of snuff-taking – he was a devoted fan of J. & H. Wilson's Special No 1 for more than half a century – Joe showed me round his ancient farm. First the big granite barns, then up the hill towards another half-hidden, overgrown barn where an old Syracuse horse plough lay, carefully tended and in good order, just as it was left when Joe last ploughed with horses: 'You could take 'im out tomorrow, just as good as he always was. The local priest had to come to me for the plough-blessing ceremony – wouldn't do with a modern plough, would it?' He laughed, and we moved on to look at an old, hand-operated winnowing machine, which Joe described in great and loving detail. 'All this was brought in in my father's time, and it worked very well so I kept it. Those big machines that do the whole lot, you know, you have to destroy the farm to get them in! And what do I want all that for? All that noise and black smoke everywhere. That's not farming, that's a sort of factory work, and it's not for me.'

The most noticeable thing about Batworthy Farm – apart from its beauty, and the intimate nature of its fields and hedges – was the clean smell: the smell of summer, and hay in the making; the smell of the small-scale enterprise; the gentle. Even the few cattle, the basis of all Joe's efforts for many years, had a quieter, less intensive aura than modern breeds.

'They're South Devons, rare animals now, but in fact just what you're supposed to have in South Devon', said Joe with a wink. 'Of course, Londoners come down and tell us to get Limosines or whatever they're called, 'cos they work out with a pencil and paper or a calculator that they can make more money with 'em, or some damn thing. No, I've always kept South Devons and I'm not changing now. They're lovely animals and as good as any other – better than most, and Father kept the same cows so the strain goes right back. Of course, other people always have to go for the fancy and foreign, but they don't really know what they're on about. They come down and tell us what to do, but I tell them if I get the chance!'

Further up the field Joe stood proudly looking over a day-old calf lying near its mother in the warm sun. We crossed that field and entered another, and Joe had names for them all: Barn Hill, Cows Flat, Barn Park – and there were many fields in spite of the fact that the farm amounted to little more than one hundred acres; but then, few of his fields were bigger than an acre or two. 'This field has eleven gates,' he told me, 'and what a useful thing that is! We can move the cows around easily and simply between one field and the next, nip in here and out there; no fuss and never far to go to get to the next gate. What's the point of huge great fields you can hardly see across – nothing but more trouble and bother, and I suppose there's money behind it.'

Another granite building once housed a stone walkway to allow a horse to go round in endless circles pulling a chaff cutter mechanism; in it, Joe showed me the cart his father once used every week to take the farm produce to market in Chagford: 'It's just as my father left it. We call it a butt cart or a tip-up cart, because' he said with a smile 'when there's no horse in the shafts it tips right over! We used to take it regularly into town till quite recently. Look what a beautiful made thing it is. Each joint in the wheels and frame hand-made.' And he was right, it was a marvellous thing, its curved sides, runner and bottom boards fitting together perfectly. Through the blister of many years' sun and rain the still sturdy cart carried the name and address, carefully inscribed, of Joe's father.

Up in another of Joe's little fields on the edge of the hillside a second small group of sad-eyed cattle flicked their tails in the heat, allowing Joe to come within inches of their noses, even though they were rather nervous, having only recently calved. The scene had all the calm dignity of farming as carried on as a living craft, rather than a business, and the cattle seemed to reciprocate this feeling of respect as they allowed Joe to pat a calf just a few days old. Joe's attitude to his animals was matched by his attitude to the appearance of the farm:

'Well, I'll give you an example of what the modern machine can do. We had one of our hedges cut with one of them flails some years ago, and it took the life out of it, made it look awful. I told them I didn't want it done ever again. I prefer the hedges well grown, not cut and slashed down into a mess, just like I prefer to leave my woodland traditional because this gives a bit of cover for the wildlife and the foxes – I used to be a great hunting man! We boys used to get out together after the old fox, and what good times we had! You need a bit of woodland for foxes. I used to love the gymkhanas, too, and used to ride the old pony over to them wherever they were, for a laugh and a bit of talk. Even going into Chagford each week was a bit of fun, because we'd meet all the other good old boys and have a yarn and an argument. But there are few of us left now, except at the Chagford Show.

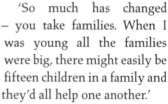

'So much has changed – you take families. When I was young all the families were big, there might easily be fifteen children in a family and they'd all help one another.'

The old ways died slowly in this part of Devon. Fuel for the range in the house and for the fires was never bought in, for example, because with plenty of well-grown hedgerows and bits of woodland dotted about the place, Joe and Annie were well able to stock up for the winter.

'There's always windfalls and we cuts a bit of timber here and there,' explained Joe, 'though you'd never notice we'd taken it. Plenty of wood hereabouts.'

Joe laughed a lot and his glorious Devon accent took some getting used to, but he was a kindly man, small and neat of stature, whose nature seemed to match the quiet of his working life. Annie, his sister, could often be found sitting on an upturned basin in the lane that ran by the farm. She returned to the farm where she had spent her childhood after her husband died; in latter days she helped with the cattle and with Joe's other great passion, his vegetable patch, where neat rows of onions and potatoes would grow quickly in the sheltered valley. 'I grow a lot of my vegetables for competitions at the Chagford Show,' he explained. 'They give prizes for the biggest onions, and the biggest leeks and carrots, though I bother mostly for the talk and the argument.' Joe and Annie were virtually self-sufficient in vegetables, and the few chickens that wandered happily about the yard provided eggs and meat. 'So we don't need much to live on, and we certainly don't need money for holidays 'cos we don't have any! I like my holidays here – after the harvest there's always a bit of time. I've never gone away from here because anywhere else it's all going too fast, and I'd get in the way with my old ideas; but I can't help thinking they're better ideas. I have names for the cows, for example, not numbers which is what the European Union is all about.

'Farming used to be a sociable thing. At harvest-time, for example, we'd press the apples and have cider

– my brother would come round and my friends, and we'd all help each other and we'd drink and talk in the fields, laugh and chat about everything. It isn't good now the way farming is carried on and I don't want to be part of it; perhaps that's why I've changed so little. People convince themselves it was all harder in the past with horses and carts and no tractors because they want to believe everything's all right now; but they know it isn't. Farming is easier, but it's worse because the life has gone out of it. Take the grass, for instance: great big mowing machines came down here with the incomers and they cut too much and killed all the lanes; and they killed all the wild pheasants and partridges in the fields because they cut twice a year. It was all just greed, factory boys on the land.

'We had the time to stop every now and then, but not any more. It's all rushing now, and making money. When I was young, if one farmer killed a lamb or a pig he'd share it with the other farmers round about; and we'd sell our butter and cream in Chagford. Now, of course, we're not allowed to sell a thing. And because of all these subsidies there are now only two cow farmers left in the Chagford area, and I'm one of them. 'Tis all wrong. People always wanted our cream for their children and at Easter – they were the great times for cream. Otherwise we fed a lot of it to the pigs. And then we'd have the pig at Christmas! We supplied the big houses, too, the gentry. It's the last ten years that have seen the biggest and the worse changes; now, for example, I've got to register every single animal, and I've got to clip the cows' ears and all sorts.'

But for Joe himself things had changed little over the decades, and if anything, he travelled less in his old age than he did as a young man. 'Well, I used to ride the pony to school as a child, and I suppose that was a bit of travelling,' he said with a smile. 'Every day I'd get up on her and trot along the lanes, though really there wasn't anything special about that, because it was how everyone got around, or in a cart. And our pleasures were all here, too, either in the fields after harvest or in the barn if it was raining; we'd have cider and we'd kill our own pigs and chickens, not the London way, I know, but how my family have done things for generations; and I don't see no reason to change it all now.'

We moved on round the farm and up the deep overgrown lane, thick with foxgloves. Joe loved the countryside in and around the farm, but he was not overly sentimental about it; he remembered the pig killer calling each year, and wringing the necks of chickens was an everyday occurrence, their feathers used in pillows and bolsters. A lack of sentimentality did not mean, however, that he had anything of the cynic about him. Cynicism he thought was for the modern farmers, those who believe that working the land is purely and simply a business, a way to make money, as he explains:

'I could make the fields bigger and get the combine in, and bother with all this EU nonsense, but why – to give me more leisure time? Leisure time for what? For going round causing trouble? No, I'm happy here doing what I've always done – or at least I was till this EU thing. I can't understand it at all. I can't take my eggs into Chagford any more to sell them; nor my milk, nor anything. I have to have my cows' ears nicked and tagged and marked, and now I have to tell people in another country exactly what every square inch of the farm grows or is used for. It's a load of nonsense; and when I filled in the forms they even told me I hadn't got the acreage right!

'As good as the day it was made,' said Joe, suddenly changing the subject; we had moved out of the sunshine into another old granite building where a chaff cutter with its great curving handle stood oiled and ready for use, as if the thirty years since it was last regularly employed had dropped away in an instant. And the roller that bruised the corn for the horses was still there, too. 'All this stuff's been here since the day I first remember anything on this farm, and my father had them a long time before he even thought of me. We last used the chaff cutter for the last horse we had in the 1960s.

'Father and I used to plough together, and before that an old boy called Frank Long worked for us, drove our horses till my brother and I were old enough. You could plough about one acre a day, which was more than enough on a small farm, and it was a lovely skilled and satisfying business when you got it right. You'd mark your line, and it was a matter of pride to get as straight a furrow as you could. We used to help the major who farmed nearby with his ploughing, too. I had two brothers and Annie, my sister, and we all worked then; I can still clearly remember the fun we had in the cornfield at harvest-time as the last bit of it was cut and the rabbits came pouring out. They were everywhere, dozens of them, hundreds sometimes – the dogs used to chase them, and the children, everyone! But there are fewer rabbits now, myxy has seen to that, and we have less corn.

'We always kept two plough horses and another one for odd work, for pulling the mangel cart and suchlike, and Father always had something decent to ride; he liked to ride, and used the horse to go about selling potatoes, and he could always stop at the pubs because they all had stables for travellers and their horses.

'I remember at harvest-time how we all helped make the ricks, and that was a real skill; but we enjoyed helping, and eating and drinking, too, in the fields as we did the work. So many farms have those big machines now that make a great roll of hay all wrapped in plastic at the touch of a button. And when we were older and the days were wet we'd sit and drink cider and talk. You'd sit with all your mates and just chat about this and that. I don't know why we enjoyed it all so much, but we did. Of course there were arguments, too, like boundaries for example – there'd be terrible rows about them, and if you put a ferret down another man's hedgerow he'd shoot you if he could!'

If Joe seemed against everything that had come into farming in his old age it was only because he considered that the changes damaged the unique local nature of his work, rooted as it was in the neighbourhood and traditions of Devon. He could never accept, and many would sympathise with his view, that rules created in Brussels to cover farms in a dozen countries and in a thousand different locations, could be a better answer than solutions and farming practices worked out locally over centuries. For Joe, a Europe he neither knew nor cared much for, was trying to tell him how to run a farm he knew better than anyone in the world. He was understandably furious. He could understand that during the Second World War it was essential that the country should pull together to grow as much corn as possible – as a result he ploughed up his pastures as instructed – but he knew that the war would end, and that he should then return his land to its traditional use as pasture. During his last years he received complex, unfathomable letters written in a style that referred to farming as if it were simply an industrial process of yields and averages, profit and loss, input and output; the distance from which the commands came and the inexplicable nature of their message struck Joe as profoundly undemocratic.

Both Joe and Annie knew that when they were gone the farm was bound to change, and that, in a very real sense, they were the last link in a chain that stretched back, in essence unchanged, to medieval times; to days when the countryside was still populated by people who were as much a part of their land as the woods and fields and pastures.

Suppliers and Consumers

A revolution which has gradually taken place during
the last fifty or sixty years has lessened the number of
suppliers and added largely to the body of consumers.
The cottagers have been driven into villages, the
villagers have been forced into towns and the
townspeople have been enticed into cities.

While the cottagers remained in their hamlets and
the villagers in their villages, they derived much of
their subsistence from the soil whereon they lived;
when they became townsmen they ceased to be partly
suppliers and began to be altogether consumers.

We owe much of this disadvantageous change to
our modern system of agriculture. This has produced
the most calamitous effects without effecting all the
salutary consequences for which it is celebrated. By
consolidating farms, by forcing cottagers from their
hamlets, by pretending to make much profit with little
labour the agricultural system has depopulated and
is depopulating the shires. The agricultural system
attempts to ape the manufacturing system which has
quite a different tendency.

George Chalmers, *An Estimate of the Comparative Strength
of Great Britain*, 1802

THE MUSICIAN OF THE FIELDS

LANCE WHITEHEAD
TENTERDEN, KENT

*L*ance Whitehead sat in his massive beamed sitting-room and talked about a farming life that is probably as close to the old ways as was possible to be in the second half of the twentieth century. He always cut his own wood for his fires in winter, tended his cattle and had no interest at all in agribusiness or in making money for the sake of it.

His house was and is a perfect example of a medieval hall house converted during Tudor times to a house with two floors, and it had hardly been touched in three hundred years by the time Lance came to live there. It had no damp course, and the baked floor-tiles in the sitting room were laid straight onto the sand; but none of this bothered him in the slightest. 'Well, the floors did sweat a bit in winter, I must admit, and rain came down the chimney, but it was warm enough so long as we burned a couple of wheelbarrow loads of logs each day!'

Lance laughed, and rocked back in his chair, which, like all the other chairs in his sitting, room, was loaded with bits and pieces of wooden furniture designed to keep his black Labrador out of them. He threw another massive log – more like half a tree – on the fire, gently clouted the dog, and then talked about his father and his long line of Kentish ancestors: 'My family first came to this house in 1942, though I was born in a tiny cottage about half a mile away, one of a number of cottages bought by my grandfather who owned the windmill at the top of the lane. The windmill was burned down in 1913, and afterwards my father bought what remained of it together with the bakehouse, the grounds and some cottages.

'When my parents got married my grandfather gave them a cottage – he was a baker, originally at a place called Wittersham about three miles from here, but my grandmother was a farmer's daughter from Biddenden, about four miles away; her family had farmed there for more than two hundred years. However, the house I live in now was built, we think, in about 1480; it is immensely higgledy-piggledy and is built entirely of oak timbers. I've lived here for fifty years.' Forstall Farm stood alone at the end of a long lane. Pasture ran almost to the door, and the house has views over the Weald that can have changed little in this peaceful corner of Kent for centuries. Lance was particularly conscious of farming as a way of life, and in his case, a way of life that went back generations:

'My wife's grandfather was a hop grower, but she came, on one side at least, from a long line of farmers. My parents moved into this ancient house on 11 October 1942, Michaelmas Day – everything in those days was sorted out, or let or rented either from Michaelmas Day or from Lady Day in March. If you went into a farm you always started at Lady Day, and you had to buy the farm and also its valuation, by which was meant the value of the work and effort already put into it, the crops already growing, the hedges laid, the fences and so on. You would judge what

had been done by walking around and looking at the state of things generally.

'Every year now you have to do the same thing for the taxman, so if you keep a few more cows you have to declare it so he can take his cut. We used to have a professional valuer in each year, but now I do it all myself.

'I was eleven when we moved here, and though Mum came from farming stock, Dad was a Londoner really. He'd been injured in the Great War and his brother had been killed; when he came back to England to recuperate he was sent down to a farm. A lot of people did the same – the appeal of good country air, I suppose – and obviously they thought that would be best for a while; but Dad must have really enjoyed it because he never went back to London. He worked on several farms, and eventually became what was known as a milk recorder; in fact he was the first one in Kent.

'Well, this job as milk recorder meant that instead of continuing as a herdsman, which is what he'd done first when he came down to Kent, he had to cycle all over the county recruiting farmers to this sort of co-operative; the idea was the forerunner of the Milk Marketing Board. However he gave it up in March 1923 and then worked for a cattle feed merchant. He was what was known then as a commission agent, that is he would go round and sell cattle, pig and poultry feed using the contacts he'd made when he'd worked as a milk recorder.'

Lance's father made a great success of this work, but World War II put paid to it because the War Department decided that all feedstuff manufacturers should be nationalised. 'I suppose it was inevitable,' said Lance with a wry smile, 'because everything was in short supply, but for us it meant that my father was out of a job. He looked around to see what he could do and decided that, as he'd been working part-time as a special constable, he should try being a regular cop. So he had a chequered career – but what all this is really leading up to is his decision to come here.

'There's a Forstall Farm in virtually every area of Kent, and I think the word means a place where things are bought and sold, a sort of unofficial market place. I think it comes from the word 'fostte' which was a place where you could buy and sell without going into the town and paying a toll at the gates.

'Anyway, the tenancy of this place came up because the couple who were farming it at the start of the second war were very old and just couldn't carry on. Lots of farms were still derelict at that time – it was particularly bad between the wars right across Britain. The War Agricultural Commission was empowered to have any ground they chose ploughed up for the war effort, and the order came through to this old couple to plough up the Big Field. They said it couldn't be done because it was in such a mess with thistles, anthills and so on; they had come to the farm in 1897 and the Big Field hadn't been ploughed in living memory. It was twenty-six acres of rough ground, although maps from 1860 show it was then split into four fields, but Mum and Dad were determined to do it when they came, so they got hold of a thing called a D2 – it was like a tank! An ordinary tractor couldn't have done the job. Some farmers had the old Fordson tractors in those days; the first Fordson was built just before the Great War, but it wasn't updated till 1944 and even then the updated model had only three gears. Anyway, we used the D2, and we got the Big Field ploughed; but even with that great tank of a thing it was tough going.

'All the mowers and binders and reaping machines were powered then by the movement of their own wheels – modern equipment has power for the wheels and power for the binder or whatever it is – so if the wheels slipped on the ground you lost power. These early machines were pulled by horses, too, so there wasn't much traction, and hence power, anyway. They were odd-looking things, too, with drive belts running all over the place.'

But even in the late 1930s and early 1940s much farm-work in Lance's part of Kent was still done by hand or with the help of horses. 'It wasn't most of the work here, it was *all* the work, or that's how it seemed. And it was only when the War Office created machinery depots that things began to change, because only then could more farmers use machines and overcome their long-standing prejudice against anything new-fangled.'

By today's standards, of course, the early pieces of mechanical agricultural equipment seem positively antediluvian, but for farmers like Lance they represented some relief from back-breaking physical labour. 'The old binders were useful but very unwieldy. They had a six-foot wide cut and were too big to go straight through a field gate; they had to be towed through sideways. A winding handle lowered the driving wheel once the thing was in position, and when you did this the wheels on which it ran were lifted off the ground; thus the machine stayed still, and we brought the corn to it. I remember when it first arrived it took us all day to work out how to set it up and use it! A big cog on the driving wheel to the main chain drove the blades and sweeps and the hay was lifted on to a canvas conveyer, and then lifted on to an elevator over the driving mechanism to the other side where it was packed into sheaves. Finally a knotter was activated. The whole thing was adjustable and you set the height according to the height of the crop. Unlike a modern combine harvester, the one we used seemed to involve men everywhere, operating levers or rushing about adjusting things.

'Before the old binders could be set going the field still had to be "opened up" by hand: a man would scythe a wide path right round the field and only then did the tractor have enough room to tow the machine round the field to harvest the rest of the crop. Like most of the smaller farms, we couldn't afford to buy a machine so we hired one each year at harvest time.'

But if agriculture had become easier just after the end of the Second World War, family life for Lance took a more difficult turn while he was still at school. 'My father just walked out one day when my brother and I were in our late teens; he just disappeared for good and we haven't seen him since. But my mother decided to carry on with the farm, and, as luck would have it, this being just after the war, she had two German prisoners of war to help. Like most prisoners who were sent on to the farms, our two were very hard-working: many stayed on for good when the war ended, and although one of ours went back to his home in 1946, the other, Heinrich, stayed on until he died in 1992.

'In 1950, three years after my father disappeared, my brother and I decided to take on the farm. We didn't really know much about running a farm, although of course we'd worked for Mother for years during school and college holidays. I still felt slightly the amateur, I suppose, because I could have had another career as a musician.' In fact Lance had studied at the Guildhall School of Music in London for a number of years. However, the pull of the land had been too strong; he disliked living in London, and was much happier back farming where science and technology were making further inroads.

'One of the great things in the late 1940s and early 1950s was the elimination of tuberculosis in herds of dairy cattle. Our cows were OK, so we decided to register the herd as an attested Tb-free herd; this was an expensive thing to do, but it meant we would be able to get more for our milk. Then everything went wrong: Mother bought a cow that seemed fine, but it died, and then the others died – they all died eventually, and it was heartbreaking. There and then we decided we would no longer buy in cows as the risk was too great. We still get occasional problems with them, but if they close you down these days because the herd is infected, at least you get compensation.'

Like most traditional farmers, Lance and his brother ran Forstall as a mixed enterprise, thus minimising the risk of overall loss should any particular part of the business suddenly drop disastrously in value in years of general over-production. 'When we first took over, my brother and I kept pigs and poultry as well as cattle, and we grew as cattle, and we grew corm.

'All our hay was turned by hand in those days. We raked it into rows having cut it using our old Fordson tractor and a converted horse mower, and eventually built it into a rick; and that was a very skilled business. First we'd put faggots – bundles of sticks – on the ground to keep the hay up off the damp soil. Then we'd work round a central pile of hay that was always kept higher than the outside edge, and gradually it would rise from the ground. The idea was to keep the rick slightly domed so the rain would run off quickly; and the theory is that each pitch of hay holds down the one below.'

That was the theory, but as Lance laughingly confessed, things didn't always go as planned and in truth a wayward hayrick could be a terror: 'We had some disasters – sometimes the rick would seem fine until you'd nearly finished it, and then almost without warning, the whole lot would begin to lean and you were in real trouble! You could prop it up if you were lucky, but one of the effects of its great weight was to exacerbate hugely any tendency to lean one way or another – and once it had started to lean it might very suddenly all avalanche into a great untidy pile. But I'm sure it happened now and then to the best of farmers.

'Sometimes when we piled the hay on the waggon it was just as bad; waggon-loads of hay weren't always those neat things you see in paintings, and you might have to pull the cart back to the rick-yard with a couple of men holding the hay in with sticks from one side. Once the rick was built, it would be given a proper thatched roof just like a house roof. The weight of hay on hay meant it would end up packed very tight, which is why chunks had to be cut out with a special hay knife. With re-seeded hay you have hollow stems, too, so after a few weeks all the hollow would be crushed out of it in the rick, and what had been ten or twelve feet high would have sunk to head height.

'When my brother and I first started here we had only a couple of house cows which supplied just our needs, but eventually we had ten or twelve milking cows and we could make a reasonable living from their milk. At one time early on we survived by selling the milk from just four cows, real subsistence stuff! It was hard work milking then, even with only a few animals, because you had to milk by hand at least twice a day and sometimes three times if you wanted the maximum yield of milk. We'd put the milk in churns and take them up to the end of the lane where they were collected by the milk lorry. It's all much easier now with tankers and sterile tanks and so on. We got our first milking machine in 1952 – it cost £150, and it's the only thing I've ever had on hire purchase! Forty years later we were still using bits and pieces of that original machine.

'We used to get up at 6am, which wasn't really early by fanning standards, and one of us would milk the cows while the other fed the calves and pigs. Then we'd go into the house for breakfast before getting out again to clean out the cowshed. If it was haymaking time we'd perhaps spend the morning turning a piece that had been mowed; we eventually stopped doing it by hand when we bought a hay-turning machine for £5! This was just a couple of wheels and a series of rakes that moved to one side and flipped the hay over – you had to turn the hay like this in the field to make sure it was dry before you took it to be ricked. Balers were only just starting to appear at this time.

'Most of our corn was grown for the cattle, though we also grew oats and beans. We kept the straw for bedding. My brother did most of the ploughing and harrowing, and then we'd both do the hoeing which was incredibly back-breaking work in the days before weedkillers – my back has never been the same since. All the planting we did by hand, and we sowed by hand, too, using a box with two handles and an iron wheel; as you pushed it along it popped the seeds out. But it was such slow, laborious work that in the end we just couldn't cope with it. All farm-work then was laborious, though. Another job we had to do every day was to make a huge pile of mangels and pulp them by hand which we then mixed with chaff and oats to feed to the cattle; they absolutely loved it, though now they get cattle cake that we buy in, and hay. Again, it just makes the work less hard for the farmer.'

Lance had happy memories of family harvests, and even in winter, farming with his brother was a sociable business – 'you're a bit lonely in one of those air-conditioned modern tractor cabs' he said – but it was very much a 24-hour a day job, with few breaks and holidays. 'There were so many things to be done in a day. Just take weeds, for example. Weeds were a terrible headache for all farmers forty or more years ago, particularly if you let them get ahead of you. That first crop we grew on the Big Field was supposed to be wheat, but it turned out to be a crop of hay, wheat and weeds in equal measure!'

'Weeds were particularly bad in this area – we used to say that we were still picking thistles out of our shins at Christmas. But although I complain about the weeds I suppose it has to be said that along with more wild flowers around, and thicker hedges, the countryside was very different back then. When I was young I loved the rooks, too, although the farmers thought there were too many of them. That sound was the sound of my boyhood, and flocks were so big you'd see them flying by for half an hour. On windy autumn days we used to watch them as they battled their way through the headwinds. They were certainly a hell of a nuisance on beans, but they ate a lot of pests too, wireworms and so on. There are far fewer now.'

Forstall Farm extends to 104 acres, of which 25 are woodland; because the woodland isn't all in one place – 'it sort of splits the land up' said Lance – 'farming it was difficult: there were ten acres of woodland roughly in the middle of the farm, another smaller wood circled a field, and there was a band of trees on the southern boundary… more a strip really, just a few yards wide,' said Lance. On the other hand, so much woodland meant there was always enough fuel for the enormous fires in the house.

If on the whole the woodland was seen as an asset, rabbits were certainly not. 'Oh, rabbits were terrible here before the coming of myxomatosis. The old couple who had the farm before we came said they lived almost entirely on rabbits. They were a cheap food for many country people, but because you could have them all the time and they were associated with the poor, most people didn't want to eat them; they just wanted to be rid of them. After myxy in the 1950s the farm was clear of rabbits for years, and we saw grass for the first time; in the pre-myxy days the rabbits would clear a field in hours – in the morning you could look out over fields that were bare that had been green the night before.

'During the war rabbits were considered so bad that the War Committee set up teams of trappers; they used gins, which are now illegal because they are so cruel, but they were very effective. The team sent down here once caught five hundred rabbits in a week, though that was probably because before the war the farm was virtually derelict and the rabbits had had a real chance to get ahead. At that time the agent said to us that Mr Holmewood, the previous tenant, managed to starve half a sheep to the acre! That's how difficult a farm it was seen to be.'

But it was for precisely this reason – a difficult farm on relatively poor soil – that Forstall was at least cheap to rent. 'We got it for just £1 per acre, though Dad was the only person prepared to pay anything at all to take it on. Most people wouldn't have looked at it rent free!'

There was little money to be made in those early years, but at least Lance and his brother were independent; and things were so bad that it was widely assumed they couldn't get worse. Also, they were allowed access to better pastures through an ancient system of grazing rights, whereby Forstall animals could be summered on distant ground. 'Lots of farms hereabouts had what they called fattening ground down on Romney Marsh, and could put their bullocks down there to fatten up during the summer. We couldn't produce the quality of the grass they had down there, and it suited the marsh farmers because we paid them for the right to graze their land.'

Although it was never likely to make them rich,

Forstall was a farm that Lance knew well; he also knew that it would at least always provide him with an adequate living; so when at last the chance came to buy it, he felt little hesitation. 'We didn't buy until 1953, and the farm had belonged to a Quaker family for centuries. We dealt with two sisters originally, Margaret and Anne Fry, though in fact before we took it on they had intended it to go to the National Trust largely because the house is so remarkable and unspoiled. When we first came as tenants even the massive, centuries-old bread oven was still here, built up against one end of the house; but we got permission from the agent to take it out, together with an old copper – it must have been hundreds of years old and would be a real rarity now, but it wasn't much use to us, and in those days things weren't considered interesting in the way they are now. However, that wasn't the way one of the sisters saw it: she thought the bread oven was a real feature, and because she wanted the house to go to the National Trust, when she discovered it had been removed the agent got a real dressing-down. Miss Fry considered we'd destroyed an important feature of the house, and I suppose we had.

'Eventually an official from the National Trust did come to look at the house, but they didn't want it, largely, I think, because it needed to have so much money spent on it. And when she found that the Trust wasn't interested in it, Miss Fry sold it to us. It was valued at £1,000 as an investment, although the valuer said that if it was sold to the tenant – ourselves, that is – a fair price would be £1,500; but Miss Fry had always had a certain sympathy for my mother's plight, so she sold it to us for £1,000. She wasn't really interested in money, so much so that she even lent us the money to buy it from her!

'Both Margaret and Anne Fry are long dead; they were unmarried and lived in London, and other than that I know nothing about them, except that they were certainly marvellous landlords. Three years before she sold the house to us, Miss Fry had a cowshed built for us which cost more than the house was worth!'

The small-scale nature of Forstall Farm was unusual even in Lance's day – 'We definitely counted as small fry!' said Lance – but even so, the days when a farmer and his family could keep going on the income from a few cows were long gone even in the 1960s. 'To make a good living you really need at least sixty cows. I had forty, and a few beef cattle. It wasn't always so, but with the rise in agribusiness and so on we were classed as a small farm, which is how I liked it. We could have increased the herd to fifty, I suppose, but bits of the farm were difficult to get to. Cows were certainly my main interest. I'd been making my living more or less solely with cows since 1950, even though in our part of Kent hops were traditionally grown; but there was little money in hops until the Hop Marketing Board started – certainly terrible trouble to make a living growing them. I think the last hops were here in the 1920s, and in fact hop growing was and is in decline all over Kent because new varieties of beer are lighter so the demand for hops has decreased.'

The life of the small farmer was almost invariably a quiet one. Lance had his animals to feed and his crops to tend; the hours were long, and as the numbers of farm-workers declined the farmer's life became increasingly become one of solitude. But Lance had hobbies and interests that took him away, however temporarily, from his secluded life:

'My great hobby was always shooting, and we used to have great days before myxomatosis. Ours were nothing like the Edwardian days on the grand shoots where they'd say about a duck or a pheasant "Up goes a guinea, bang goes a penny and down comes half a crown!" – we just used to get together with all the farmers round about for vermin shoots as we called them. We'd shoot rabbits, jays, magpies and so on; it was our bit of fun and way of socialising, because it's very difficult for a farmer to take a holiday, as you can imagine. I did try it once or twice but it doesn't work well. You have to get someone in to do the work, but he won't know your animals, won't know what each animal is fed, and when and how, so you have to give him a list of what needs doing and it's all very hit and miss. You worry when you're away, and usually you have to sort it all out when you get back!'

The solitude of farming increased for Lance when, quite amicably, he parted from his brother in the early 1950s. 'When my brother married we knew the farm couldn't manage all of us, so I bought him out. He moved to the Isle of Wight to farm, but my son Bruce helped me and will eventually take over the farm. He studied at the Royal Agricultural College at Cirencester, but mucked in during the holidays. Things were always difficult on a small, traditionally run place like ours, with not a great deal of land and only a few animals.

'My other son, Giles became an artist. I remember my daughter Tabitha had to walk two miles each day to school in Tenterden, but she helped around the place when she could. I suppose I was one of the few remaining subsistence farmers – I saw it as a way of life; a way to make a living. I never saw it as a business as bigger farmers do.

'My wife was heavily involved in farming; she was originally from Sheffield, and she died in 1990. She was captain of the Tenterden bellringers before she married me! I suppose we had music in common – I never gave up playing the cello. I played in two local orchestras at Cranbrook and Hastings. And two nights a week every week, and one additional night I played in a string quartet. So there's plenty to do and I was always kept out of harm's way!'

Lance had no regrets about the road he took in life, despite the fact that he could easily have opted for the life of a musician. 'My cello teacher studied with Pablo Casals so I was well taught, but my first love has always been the farm, which diversified a bit when my wife decided to breed Labradors – they were very good, too, and she used to sell them all over the world. They won lots of prizes in field trials and so on.

'But just to go back to shooting for a minute, I should say that I started with Dad who used to go out every Tuesday after Ashford Market. My very earliest memories are the smell of a wet dog and of Dad cleaning his gun in the evening.'

Lance kept Guernsey cows because milk was paid for on the basis of its quality and Guernsey milk is very high quality indeed. Gone were the days when all milk was paid for at a flat rate regardless of quality; although, as Lance explained, other than keeping the right animals, there was never much you could do about it: 'The quality of your milk depends to a large extent on the sort of land you've got – in other words, it depends on the soil. After decades of spreading dung on our land we've improved it a great deal, and it is now very good quality, producing marvellous grass; but it wasn't like that when we first came. We're on what's known as Wadhurst clay here, but we're only just on it, and in fact it isn't that good anyway unless it's well looked after, as we've looked after it. It's a sort of marginal area almost on the marsh – Romney Marsh, that is.

'Our woods were also difficult – difficult to coppice I mean, because much of the woodland grew in steep gills; but we always cut our own firewood and we had plenty of chestnut for fence-posts. Chestnut is marvellous, and will last for twenty years or more even if the ground is wet. It also makes wonderful roof timbers. Ash and hornbeam, by contrast, will rot in the ground in a year.'

Lance had a long list of the people who farmed at Forstall before his family arrived, but in spite of its length the list encompasses merely a third of the life of the farm, going back only to 1726: in that year it was owned by one William Finch, who also owned a farm at the other end of the lane – by 1726, of course, Forstall was already well over two hundred years old. But as far as Lance was aware it had always been a farm, even when, in the late 1400s, it was just a massive draughty hall with the smoke curling out through a hole in the roof: 'There was some ancient blackening on the roof timbers,' he explained, 'and it is believed that they didn't even have a hole in the roof; they just hoped the smoke would gradually work its way through the thatch, as of course it would; and I suppose that although it would have been cold – as there was no first floor – the smoke would at least have billowed around and gathered well above the heads of the people down on the ground. The chimneys were probably put in perhaps a hundred years after the hall was built.'

Lance made his way up the massive oak staircase, with its treads of solid carved triangular pieces of oak, and across the ancient floors, through rooms that seemed to double back on themselves. Then suddenly he was descending another staircase in a completely different part of the house. There was hardly a straight wall to be found anywhere, but the massive wall and roof beams have survived. "I sometimes think they will outlive us all,' said Lance.

Farming by Experiment

But the world is now grown so incredulous that they cannot believe that a man will become bald by being shaved at the wrong time of the moon, without more experience has been made of it for these 1,700 years past. If all these phantasies delivered down to us from the ancients be looked on as mere fables why should we acquiesce in following a pretended maxim which, though it has deceived some part of the world a great while, doth, when brought to the test of experiment prove fallacious. The experience of 1,700 years no more proves a practice to be right than the long experience of cattel drawing by their tails proved that practice right, before drawing by traces was by experiment proved to be better; for nothing can be depended on as experience, which has not been tried by experiment.

Jethro Tull, *Horse-hoeing Husbandry*, 1829

A Light at Night

I will show you how to keep fire a long while light with a little charge. Suppose you dwell in a lone farmhouse, where one is sick and you have but one farthing candle in the house and borrow you cannot and you would fain have it burn a whole long winter's night; then do thus. Cut your candle in two pieces, light one of them; heat a great pin and thrust it into the great end of the candle long-wise half the pin's length. Then fill a pail of water so deep that the candle, pin and all, will not reach bottom. Let it down into the water till it comes to the flame, there staying it awhile till the water be still; then take away your hand so still as it burns the water will raise it and which answers the whole business that the fire will go no otherways save upward to his own element.

George Atwell, The Faithfull Surveyour, 1663

$\mathcal{A}$ Marshman, Born & Bred

Richard Body
ROMNEY MARSH

'*W*hen I was young, before the Great War, we mostly grew peas, long-pod beans and turnip seed for the seed merchants. This was an excellent area for that sort of thing, along with a small part of Essex and a great deal of Lincolnshire, the reason being that each of these areas has less than the normal amount of rainfall.

Turnips and beans were all sown by hand then, and it was very hard work, I can tell you. And of course we didn't have the chemicals and sprays that are used today – in fact we weren't so active at all when it came to pests; we just accepted that they were there and treated them as best we could, but we were only able to use the techniques we'd inherited from our forefathers.'

Richard Body's Hope Farm lay on the very edge of that most haunting part of England, Romney Marsh, down at the southernmost tip of Kent and just a few miles from the ancient unspoiled towns of Rye and Winchelsea, towns virtually untouched by modern development. He was born in 1904 and remembered with the utmost clarity growing up on a remote marsh farm; and as he proudly declared, he was almost born on the marsh itself, something that had a special meaning for him and others like him:

'The marsh is like no other place in Britain. It has its own traditions and ways, and at one time it had a lot of words of its own, almost its own language. I grew up at St Mary's and I still have the letter my grandfather wrote, offering £30 a year for 300 acres of arable land in the parish. Then another letter written soon after explained that money was rather tight and withdrew the offer – my grandfather was a shrewd man! It took two more years before the family finally took the farm in 1898.'

Richard was a keen historian of local affairs, though as he explained, much of the history both of his family and of the marsh had been handed down by word of mouth. But the Bodys had certainly been farmers for generations: 'My aunt told me that the Body family came originally from Cornwall, probably early in the 1700s; and I've been able to trace the family back to 1780, to East Sussex. Though we were mostly farmers there is a record, from about 1715, of a Body from Westfield just outside Hastings and a direct ancestor of mine, who was apprenticed to a clockmaker. The family moved from East Sussex into Kent some time in the nineteenth century, to the Isle of Oxley and to Wittersham where distant members of the family live to this day. Most of Bodys have left farming now; only my family and that of a cousin are still on the land.'

Much of the land on the edge of the marsh was originally allowed to flood in winter to help provide early grass for farmers further inland, for their summer grazing; until relatively recently the marsh farmers still called these men hill farmers. Shepherds on the marsh are still called lookers by the local people; in the past the lookers were paid so much an acre per year.

Hope Farm, where Richard stayed on after retiring from active farming, is on the old sea wall, far inland from the present main sea defences. However, over the centuries floods and storms had caused shifts in the sea defences, and even in the course of the local rivers: 'Originally the River Rother reached the sea near Hythe,' he explained, 'but it silted up and was diverted to reach the sea at Romney. Then in the thirteenth century a massive storm upset everything and the course of the river returned to Rye. There have been so many changes to the area over the centuries; and millions of years ago mile upon mile of forest grew here. Now and then we used to plough up the fossilised trunks of the trees buried in the peat.

'I was born in 1904, at the farm my grandfather had taken over at St Mary's and which my father managed from about 1900. I've still got a list of the prices we paid for all the tackle we took over, the carts and waggons, drills and ploughs. None of that gear had changed much in centuries – a medieval farmer would have been quite happy to have used what we had!'

Richard had fond memories of those far-off days, but equally he had no illusions about them: 'Crops were dealt with in a different way in those days because everything was done by hand, and it was laborious. All crops were sold by the bushel, which was a measure of volume, not weight: this meant that when you filled a bag with corn you had to be careful about the way you did it – if you did it badly, the corn would sink too far into the bag and you'd have to put more in. There was a special skill in filling a bushel sack properly so that buyer and seller were happy that they'd exchanged a fair amount. If the corn was damp it had to be turned by hand to dry it, and that, like most farm jobs, was back-breaking work. When corn was threshed it was always by four-bushel sacks. Sacks were so important in those days that merchants and farmers who didn't have their own used to hire them from firms whose business it was to hire them out; there was, I recall, such a company up in London in Tooley Street called Starkie Room.

'If you sent Starkie a postcard on the Monday saying how many sacks you wanted, they'd be at Romney station the next day, or at most a day after that. There were two goods trains a day arriving at the station at that time and every passenger train had a couple of goods waggons attached. There is no railway now. Crops were sold in what probably seem odd amounts now; corn, for example, was always sold by the quarter – that is, two sacks containing eight bushels.'

The train was probably the greatest boon to the farmer early in the twentieth century because, from its heyday in the 1880s, it had spread to all but the most remote corners of the land, and Romney Marsh was well served. 'Oh yes, sheep or cattle loaded at 8am on the Romney train on a Tuesday would be at the main station at Ashford by 10am. It was a marvellously efficient service,' said Richard.

'On the farm we had big, high-sided carts for moving things around, and the normal allowance for pulling was one horse per ton load. Each district made its own style of waggon, and there were different types for different conditions: narrow-wheeled carts were used in dry weather, and broad-wheeled ones when it was wet to prevent the cart getting bogged down in the mud.

'There was a waggon-maker at Ashford, but we always bought ours second-hand, as did most of the farmers; I remember I paid £4 for one once, during the lean years of the 1920s. Our waggons had poles sticking up vertically along the sides, and we called them standards. The poles held the load in, and you could then pile up the hay or corn or whatever much higher than the sides of the waggon without the risk of it toppling out all over the place.'

Like most men of his generation Richard's family did not escape the effects of the Great War, and though he was too young to serve himself, two of his uncles were killed. Their histories, like those of Richard's parents and grandparents, have been meticulously recorded.

'My grandfather was born in Sussex, though soon after the family moved to Wittersham; that would have been in the 1860s. My grandfather had seven sons and four daughters and he was determined his sons would have a good education, so much so that he rented a farm near Sevenoaks simply to ensure that they were close enough to a school to get there each day by pony and trap.'

On leaving school, Richard's father took to farming immediately – 'it was in his blood, I suppose,' said Richard; and by this time Grandfather Body had done well and expanded his interests: 'As well as Honeychild's, the farm at St Mary's, Granddad also had a mill at New Romney and odd bits of ground here and there; he was a very shrewd man who bought and sold bits of land continually, usually at a profit. Eventually my father bought Haffenden Farm at St Mary's, which we'd leased at first, though by the 1920s things were pretty grim whatever sort of farm you were on. To give you an example of how farm produce lost its value, in 1920 wheat was sold for two shillings a sack – by 1930 that price was exactly the same, but everything else had gone up enormously in price.'

In spite of hard times the seasonal farming year remained the same; the land still had to be tilled and sown, and of course harvested: 'The main work on a farm in the summer was, without question, harvesting; it was hard work, and of course almost all by hand. But when the sun shone and you were working with people you knew well, the time passed quickly and happily.'

With the coming of winter there were ditches to be cleared and repair work to be done about the farm. There was also the back-breaking task of reed-cutting, as Richard recalled. 'The reeds grew in and along the ditches, but marsh reed isn't like Norfolk reed, which is cut when the flag is off. We cut it in winter and then stored it carefully to thatch corn- and hay-stacks, and even cottages.

'After the Great War we had some rather unusual help on the farm in the shape of two ex-army mules; one was a shocking kicker, but they were incredibly hard-working. I'll give you an example of what I mean: we had a lot of rough, thistly ground in the early 1920s, so we got a man to come and help us mow it. There was a mule, and two horses, and it was the horses that had to be rested now and then – the mule kept going without a break all day!

'In a small way my grandfather was a rather famous man because he was responsible for the "official" recognition of one of the great agricultural products of Romney Marsh: its wild white clover. It began when he entered an example of his grass in a trial; trials and competitions for the best silage, or corn, or grass seed were always being held in those days. White clover's great advantage is that although it isn't either particularly prolific or early, it is wonderfully long-lasting.'

Fairs and agricultural competitions of one sort or another, and particularly ploughing matches, made a break from what could sometimes seem to be a monotonous life; but there were other occasional entertainments. 'I remember the astonishment of the local people when one day in the 1920s a plane taking part in a Hendon-to-Paris flying race landed here – at that time hardly anyone had ever seen a plane, and the marsh was a place of quiet lanes where even cars were a rarity. The plane had had to make a forced landing and Dad helped re-start the engine, except the propeller blade nearly took his head off!'

Back on the farm the difficulties of everyday life seem astonishing by modern standards, and services which nowadays we take for granted were simply not available. 'One of the hardest jobs on the farm was getting water where it was needed because we had to carry it everywhere in buckets – for the pigs, the cattle, the thresher. We took buckets down to the pond and simply dipped them in. The work was so hard that when I was at school in Hastings I put on weight every term, and then lost it when I came back to the farm in the holidays.

'Soon after my father came back from the Great War he took me away from school early for the harvest. There were terrible rainstorms, for days and weeks on end or so it seemed, and a great part of the wheat was drowned and lost. I remember putting the sheaves into the waggon and the water pouring out through the sides as the waggon slithered and bumped along the track.'

When the time came for Richard to leave school there were family discussions about what he might do, but farming seemed the natural choice. 'I don't think I'd ever really thought much about doing anything else; it just seemed to be in my blood. Haffenden Farm was sold by my father in 1924 for a profit, and, soon after, he moved to Hope Farm. It was an old wooden house which had sunk and subsided until it was incredibly crooked – the bedroom floor had a fall from one side to the other of about four inches! And downstairs it had earth floors, which caused the house to be so badly infested with vermin that one year a rat stole my father's teeth! Hope, or Jemmet Farm as it was called, was probably built in the 1500s, but we pulled it down in the 1960s – in 1967, to be precise – as it was really beyond repair.

'In 1929, at my mother's suggestion, my father set me up on my own; it was a bad time to start, but we were optimistic that things would eventually get better. In fact I doubled my stock between 1929 and 1932, but it was worth precisely the same. My father offered me £5 a week and a share of the profits, but there were no profits in the late 1920s and early 1930s and that £5 went gradually down to £4, then £3, then £2 10s. But compared to many people we were lucky, of course, because things like eggs and potatoes didn't cost us anything.'

In spite of those dreadful early years Richard never thought of leaving the land, perhaps because his father had always encouraged his children to think well ahead and in the long term Richard knew things would get better. Also his father had done very well in other ventures, particularly in buying up plots of land and re-selling them at a small profit, so that at times they were pretty well off.

Mechanisation was slowly but surely taking its toll of traditional marsh practices, although one or two mechanical aids had been around for a very long time: 'In this area we had the right sort of ground to use the early steam ploughs and threshers. There were half a dozen or more sets of steam tackle that toured the marsh and beyond; individual farmers hired the tackle for as long as they needed it, and were charged £1 per acre. However, my father was always keen on new things and liked to be in control of his own farm and its equipment, so by 1922 he had bought his own steam plough tackle; until the late 1930s we still had horses for ploughing, partly because at one stage, although we had a steam plough we couldn't find a driver for it! The earliest steam plough down here probably arrived in the 1850s.

'A steam plough had two parts, and you'd set up one at each side of the field; then the plough was drawn back and forth between the two pieces of machinery using pulleys and conveyors. The steam plough machine itself didn't move.' Steam ploughs were cumbersome and expensive, however, so horses were still used wherever and whenever they could make a better job of it.

'We used the horses to plough in winter the ground we couldn't plough in summer, and we had two four-horse teams – this was four-horse team ground because it was too heavy for a two-horse team. Horses could plough about an acre a day, and it was a very skilled business if you were to get it right and even, with the furrows all in line and allowance left for drainage. There was a waggoner and a mate for each team and they had to cut their own chaff for their horses every evening. A steam plough could do ten acres a day compared to one for a horse team, so you can see the advantage they had; but this ground is pretty stiff, and maybe elsewhere horses did more.

'On the stiffish land down here you needed a lot of tackling – that is, equipment – for the horses. We had a balance plough for three or four horses pulling in line; a wooden jack plough for wet conditions, and a baulk plough for ridging land; a cultivator for moving ploughed ground or cleaning ground; a heavy harrow for breaking up ground with three or four horses; a three-horse corn binder, ring and flat rolls and so on. Everything was horse-driven, mowing machines, everything.'

'Mainly we used two types of plough with the horses, the balance plough which was iron, and the jack plough which was all wood except for the tip of the plough share and which had no wheels. We used the jack plough when the ground was very wet because it was lighter, and so didn't get bogged down as easily as the iron balance plough. Every part of the country had its own distinctive design of plough – for example, on the hills just off the marsh they used a plough with two wheels that was very different from anything used on the marsh. It is interesting, too, that the balance and jack ploughs we used are almost identical to ploughs I have seen illustrated in books about medieval farming!

'In 1921 we got our first telephone, but there was hardly anyone else to ring! The corn merchant had a phone so we used to call him, and it was a remarkable thing to use when it was so new and inexplicable! We shared our

line with a local sheep and cattle dealer; his number was 277 and ours was 277x!'

If farming was tough for those who had land, it was even tougher for the farm labourers who could not find regular work. There were many, particularly during the 1920s and 30s, who could only get work by travelling the country looking for seasonal employment such as tidying up hedges and clearing out ditches in winter, and perhaps helping with the harvest in summer. 'Dad helped a lot of itinerant labourers, men who used to tour the country looking for farm work; in fact he helped many get started on their own land – he'd buy a bit of land, build a little house on it and then sell it to one of these wandering labourers. In the winter, gangs of men would come round offering to clear our ditches, which was all done with shovels until the mid-1920s when we had the use of drag lines.'

Like his father, Richard is fascinated by the history of the area; and Romney has a complex history of land tenure and jurisdiction, much of which survived well into the twentieth century. 'I am lord of the manor of Ruckinge' said Richard with a chuckle. 'It doesn't mean a great deal, but Dad bought it in 1921 for £50, and I inherited it when he died. I don't think he bought it to increase his standing in the area or anything like that, because the lordship originally conferred more obligations than privileges – along with the bailiffs and jurats of the level of Romney Marsh we, the lords, were traditionally responsible for administering the drainage of the area and looking after the sea wall. We've lost all our responsibilities now, but we still meet each year on the Thursday of Whitsun week, at the hall in Dymchurch, and there is just enough money still coming in from let property to pay for our lunch!'

Romney Marsh is the only part of England that elects its own magistrates: four annually from the jurats, who are themselves elected from the local people. There are twenty-three lordships in this part of Kent, eight or nine of which are actually in the marsh; the lordships themselves go back more than a thousand years. The level of agricultural wages also made Romney Marsh unusual: 'Many people, and farm-workers in particular, liked to work on the marsh because traditionally we paid 6d or a shilling a week more than was paid in other areas. But there were disadvantages: what people used to call the ague, a kind of malaria, was always bad here because of the damp and the water, although until well into the twentieth century you could buy laudanum in the local shops to treat it. Laudanum is a kind of opium derivative and it was the only thing that would alleviate the terrible effects of the mosquitoes, before the development of a chemical antidote. We did have another experiment to control the mosquitoes – a chap introduced some kind of Hungarian frog which multiplied and thrived – you still find them everywhere – and they reduced the numbers of mosquitoes dramatically.

'Under our ground here at Hope Farm we have peat; I remember a well dug for me in 1937 produced water the colour of tea! We didn't get mains water here until 1947, and we kept horses until the last war, not as late as in some places.'

Changes in the Romney Marsh countryside in general were probably greater even than those changes to agricultural practice on the marsh farms. Roads were widened and new houses built, and cars were seen more often, although Richard was adamant that the Second World War brought the greatest changes. 'We had to plough up our pastures as part of the war effort,' he recalled, 'and somehow in the years following the war the number of men working on the land diminished as more and more improvements were made to machinery and chemicals. We once employed ten men full time; by the 1970s we didn't employ anyone. We had a chap who worked with a horse and waggon for carting and fetching wurzels, another who looked after the sheep, and a third who drove the vanner, a lighter waggon that we used for general farm work with a horse that could trot a bit and pull three-quarters of a ton on the level. We also had a thatcher here full time and a stacker, for the haystacks.

'We had two rows of cottages where the farm-workers lived, and at Haffenden Farm, which my father bought in 1912, we tried to improve the workers' rooms which were in the attic. These had plastered walls and a partition to keep male and female workers apart, but not a single window. We put windows in, though by today's standards conditions were still pretty awful for both the house-servants and farm-workers.'

Richard was the first to admit that his family was luckier than most: 'The Bodys have always had money and land, though times have been difficult now and then' he said; much of this was inherited, in particular from his grandfather's wife for whom land was kept in trust until she was old enough to take it on. In their belief in the value of land, even during the difficult 1930s, the Bodys were typical of many ancient yeoman farmer families. And in his youth, Richard certainly knew ways and methods that his ancestors would have understood. 'Decisions were always made slowly and judgments were based on experience, not scientific measurement. For instance, a corn merchant in the old days would test a sample of corn by hand and by smell alone. These days they use machines to test for moisture content and all sorts.

'Before the Great War, little had changed for centuries. For example, I have a letter written about a Romney Marsh farmer in 1786, and the practices it describes are just the ones I remember, more or less. We still drove the sheep along the roads as they did then, though not quite so far. This is the writer's description of how the sheep went to market:

"Soon after lambing is over they begin to draw off their old sheep that were set on to fattening the Michaelmas before. They are generally sent some in the wool, some out of the wool, as the season advances, to the London market, which is about 70 miles off, by Drovers who make that their employment. They are nearly a week in going, travelling at about the rate of 14 miles a day and are consigned to some particular salesman in Smithfield market. The salesman receives them off the drover at some place in the neighbourhood of London. He has them to the next market at Smithfield, two of which are held weekly, on Mondays and Fridays; he sells them to the carcase butchers and writes by that day's post to the owners informing them to whom he has sold them and at what price and deducting expenses of droving and selling which comes on the whole to about 1 / shilling a head. The grazier draws for the money which is paid at sight, so that he himself has no trouble whatever in the business. There are other smaller markets on this side of London called as the Lower Markets where they sometimes send their fatting sheep – i.e. Tunbridge, Maidstone and Rochester. In these markets the drovers are the salesmen who take and bring home the money to their employers and if any of the sheep tire on the road they sell and account for them."

For Richard, records like this from the end of the eighteenth century are not much different from his own memories of life on the marsh early in the twentieth century. 'If it was a real wet day the waggoner or his mate took the horses that needed shoeing to the forge where, of course, others would have gathered for the same reason; so there would be a queue. I can remember the men standing in under the covered part of the building out of the rain, but with their shoulders protected by sacking. They always enjoyed it because they could have a good old chat while they waited.

'Another important job for the waggoner was to grease all the waggon-and cart-wheels. This was normally a two-man job. The carts were great heavy things and each wheel had to be jacked up in turn. The lynch-pin was then taken out with what we called a lynch-pin drawer, a T-shaped tool with a claw that slid along the round, half-inch shaft. This claw hooked under the head of the pin, and in the nave or hub of the wheel there was always a 2in square gap on the outer edge to allow the pin to be pulled right out. The wheel was then slid off the axle and a good layer of thick cart grease, made from horse and other animal fats, was smeared on to the top part of the axle. The wheel would then be lifted back onto the axle in such a way as to leave as much grease as possible on top of the axle. Then the inside edge of the pin had to be greased and driven back into its hole in the axle. Before the jack was lowered the wheel was carefully spun to distribute the grease evenly. I remember the grease was always either thick black or a dirty yellow colour. Before the job was finished it was important that the lock was greased; this was the part on which the shafts turned, and if it wasn't well greased the horses would find it difficult to turn the cart.

'If he was travelling hilly country it was the waggoner's responsibility to take a skidpan with him: this was used to prevent the waggon from running away with a heavy load as it went downhill. For hilly country the waggoner would also need to be properly equipped for holding his waggon if the horses needed a "blow" – a breather – when going up the hill. Sometimes a wooden block would be used for this, but better still was a wooden roller about six inches in diameter; this would be hung behind the rear near wheel. Waggons were never fitted with brakes. At the bottom of a hill you had to be very careful when you took the skidpan off because it would be burning hot from the friction of the road – many a man received a bad burn by forgetting this.

'Another wet-day job was collecting stones from the beach to mend the farm roads. The waggons would go down to New Romney Corporation Beach Hole, as it was known, situated on the St Mary's Bay road; a one-horse waggonload would cost you sixpence, a two-horse waggonload a shilling. Men going out on these wet days would be dressed with a sack tied across the shoulders, and another sack with one corner pushed in to make a hood to stop the rain going down their backs.

'The waggoner would cut the hay for his horses straight from the stack using an extremely sharp hay-knife: this would be honed periodically, along with all the other farm blades – like those on the chaff-cutter – on the farm grindstone.

'Other men might be employed

during bad weather to make bonds: these were used to tie the straw as it came out of the threshing machine. Bonds were the only thing available for tying trusses of hay or straw until factories started to make hemp, sizal or jute-twine at a reasonable price. They were made of strong oat straw or tough hay, and they were worked by two men, a bondmaker – the skilled bit – and a turner. The bondmaker would hold a strong bunch of straight hay, then the turner would hook a wimble, a sort of twisting device, over the hay and begin to turn; the bondmaker would gradually add more hay to the bundle in his hand until a long thick rope had been produced. A five-foot bond was needed for a 28lb truss of straw. The bondmaker would stand by his pile of hay as the bond was made, while the turner moved gradually away as its length increased. When a bond was finished the turner folded both ends together and left it aside until perhaps fifty were ready to be bundled up together. Because of the friction involved by the twisting bond, the bondmaker always wore a thick leather hand-guard, usually made from an old piece of boot leather. In a fair day's work two men might make 900 bonds; for one day's threshing you would probably need 1,200 bonds.

'The great standby in really bad weather was sack-mending. Wherever the sacks were hung in a barn the rats and mice were always able to find them, nest in them and make holes in them! Sacks were to carry four bushels; some were made of soft jute, others of a cotton and jute mix – these were the best sacks. Soft balls of string called fillis were used to mend the sacks, though binder twine was an alternative, and there was a real skill to the business. A needle with a curved, flattened and extremely sharp tip was used to make a ring of loops round the edge of a hole; then another slightly smaller series of loops was joined to that first ring, and so on until the hole filled. You couldn't do it the way you'd darn socks or it would have no strength at all.'

Richard remembered the pleasure farm work could give, but he was keenly aware, too, of just how hard life could be: 'I can remember feeding hay to our cattle in about 1917. Each cow was fed the right amount for her particular needs, and of course like the water, the feeding was sorted out by hand. We called the chunks of feed-hay "cants", and these were cut by hand, about three feet wide and two feet across, I suppose. You used your two-pronged fork to lift a cant of hay high on to your shoulders, and then you'd stagger under the load into the cattle yard. It was very hard work and the least wind would throw you off balance. And in the cold it was dreadful work.

'All hay buyers carried with them an iron rod about six feet long with a barb near the tip. The rod was pushed right into the haystack, and when it was pulled out again the barb would be hanging on to a small sample from the centre of the stack. The idea was that the buyer could then see and smell what the stack was really like in the middle. The rod was also used to test if the stack was too hot: if it had been stacked too green or too damp the hay could get so hot that it would very likely burst into flames. If the rod came out and the end was too hot to touch – which did happen – then the buyer knew that the stack had reached the danger point and had to be turned or the centre cut out.

'Pebbles and stones from the beach were used to surface all the marsh roads until long after the Great War ended, and indeed on the smaller lanes it continued to be used until after the Second War. Macadam – not tarmacadam, it's not the same thing at all – came into use at the end of the nineteenth century: rock was brought down into the marsh from Lympne or Aldington and then broken up into small pieces by elderly men wearing wire gauze glasses. This broken rock would be spread over the road to be re-surfaced and then well steam-rollered to make it level. A certain length of the beach lanes would be macadamed each year: in summer in the heat these roads grew white and dusty, in winter they turned into a sea of white mud.

'It was only after the Great War that the roads gradually became tarred, and it was a slow process; before that the white roads would be gradually rutted by the iron-clad wheels of the carts, and the grass would grow in the deep ruts and in the worn centre of the road where the horses' hooves gradually broke the surface. Until the roads were tar-sprayed and gritted with crushed stones from the beach, every village had its own roadman who would be out every day throughout the long winter scraping the mud from the ruts.

'I remember, too, the last working windmill here: the Romney Mill, which stopped turning in 1916. It was pulled down in 1920, and there was a lot of interest when the auction was held because of the pitch-pine timbers from which the mill had been built.'

It is difficult to comprehend how poor the mass of people in the countryside were in the first part of the twentieth century. Sticks were gathered by the women for firewood, and after the corn had been harvested, by ancient custom the gleaners would come into the field, poor women and children who gathered up odd scraps of corn to feed their families. They would go into the pastures, too, to collect scraps of wool that the sheep had shed. According to Richard this practice lasted well into the 1930s, and the richest pickings were to be had round the sheep pound: 'A good gleaner could collect a fair old bundle of good wool in a day,' he remembered.

But at the centre of rural and agricultural life was the horse, whether used for the heavy work of tilling and cultivating the land, or for the more delicate business of transporting the farmer and his family. All the Body children were taught to ride, but for special journeys they would travel in the trap, a lightweight two-wheeled affair open to the elements, but with room for two adults and two children.

'I remember one incident to do with traps and horses, at harvest-time, probably about 1910. The gypsies were in the fields bean-cutting – they arrived year after year asking for work – and one of the gypsy men was going to the far end of the farm in a dung cart, so I asked for a ride. No one saw me go, and there was such a hue and cry when it was discovered that I was missing ... When I got back I was in disgrace, and sent to bed without any tea!'

'At Honeychild's, the farm we had till 1911, there was stabling for two teams of four working horses. Adjoining the house there was also stabling for three light horses, together with a carriage house and, over it, groom's quarters. In 1913 we moved into Haffenden where we also had two four-horse teams, and a vanner and at least two trap horses which were used in the best trap. We had a big, square market cart, too. One vivid memory from those very early days is of being put in charge of the front horse of the three that drew the binder at harvest-time. I sat on the high up on that great horse most of the time, in spite of the heat, and I remember my legs got dreadfully burnt – I've been shy of the sun ever since! Another early job for me was to keep the horse that worked a straw or hay elevator going forwards. The horse had to keep going all day around a 20ft diameter circle – some horses didn't mind this at all, but others would keep stopping.'

The technique for schooling and breaking horses had been handed down from one generation to another, and it had to be done carefully and slowly if it was to produce a well behaved, enthusiastic working animal. The process started simply by getting the waggoner's lad to lead the young horse until it would do it easily. Then it would be led with harness on. Finally it would be chain harnessed to a cart as the middle of three horses in line. The horse behind and the one in front would be good, steady animals used to the work, and kept in check by these old stagers the new horse, in the middle, would more or less have to behave, although two men would normally walk one on either side of it.

'From 1930 onwards tractors began to take over most of the work,' recalled Richard. 'And I remember how sad it was when one of our last horses got out on the road late one night in 1939 and was killed by a lorry.'

Richard had many happy memories of his early farming life, although he accepted that many of the old ideas about looking after and training animals would be considered cruel today. 'I remember a chap called John Hooker who took over Honeychild's Farm in about 1921. One of his farm horses was a jibber, in other words every now and then it would refuse to pull a load. So Hooker hitched it to a cart with half a load of straw in it, and the man in charge then put a small pile of straw under the horse's belly and set it alight! The horse went forward all right, but only far enough for its own comfort: it stopped with the burning straw under the cart, and the whole lot went up in flames!'

Fire may have been useful under these circumstances, but at a time when the fire service was at best rudimentary, the fear of domestic fires was very real. 'In 1920 the Flying Field at Jesson had been mown for hay, and early one evening there was a phone call to say that the stack was burning. The Lydd fire brigade was called for – then the only fire brigade in the marsh – and in the meantime we dipped buckets into a ditch and passed them along a human chain to keep the fire under control. An hour or so later the brigade arrived to a great cheer, but at a walk! They were exhausted, having started off at a full gallop and come seven miles.

'Two or three dung carts were able to move some of the burning hay which had been cut off the stack into the middle of the field. Much was saved out of the core of the stack, and pressed and sent by rail for the London horses, but we lost a lot of valuable hay, too.'

Heavy reliance on laudanum and other opium derivatives, which could be bought freely in local shops until well into the 1950s, may have helped the marsh people survive the damp airs and malaria, but it undoubtedly also contributed to their eccentricities. And the situation was no doubt further exacerbated by the isolation of many of the smaller marsh communities. 'There were some marvellous odd characters in and around the marsh in those days. I remember Miss Banks, the retired schoolteacher. We once found a horse's skull in her house, and although she was

a portly woman she used to pedal into New Romney to do her shopping on a tricycle pulled by a big collie dog.

'Then there was Miss Richardson who kept her bedroom absolutely full of canaries. There were hundreds of them. She never liked my father, who only had one eye – she once threatened to poke out his other eye with a hat pin!

'Then there was Tom Else, who was quite old when I knew him fifty years ago; he was our odd-job man. He'd been kicked badly by a horse when he was young, and as a result was very lame. He started working for us at Michaelmas in 1912. The hiring of men, the leasing of land and so on all began on Michaelmas Day then. Tom used to pump the water for us from a well every day, and he'd drive the trap, too. He and I must have put many tons of hay on the London waggon over the years.

'Trib Boulden was a steam-plough foreman and odd-job man with a real talent for engineering. He used to fix the first cars that arrived down here and he was a real craftsman – I remember he made me a lovely chisel from a half-inch thick piece of raw metal. He helped to repair the carriages, too. Trib was born and lived his whole life in the same village. He always had a bottle of cold tea with him, and even in his sixties, which was when I knew him, he could lift two half-hundredweights over his head, one in each hand.

'Albert Dennis was a quiet man who served right

through the Great War. He was a master stack builder, and what I particularly remember about him was that the skin of his hands was incredibly hard – he could handle any sheaves of corn without gloves, no matter how full of sharp thistles they were. He was a real expert worker but no horseman, though he could do just about anything else – dibbing in long-pod beans, planting turnips and so on, and he was always the man we got to mow by hand around the field before we could bring in the binder for a clear first round. He always wore leather straps around his trousers just below the knees; his trousers looked baggy as a result but they wore out more slowly, or so he claimed.

'Then there was Will Blacklock of Lydd; as well as Lydd land, William had a farm at Newchurch and in earlier times he used to walk from Lydd to Gammon's Farm, a distance of seven miles, to be there for 6.30am to set the men to work; then he'd walk back to Lvdd in time for breakfast! He was a leading member of the local coursing club in the 1920s and used to carry a long plank with him on coursing days – the idea was that wherever he went across the marsh he could always get across any ditch or drain by throwing his plank down in front of him!

'John Hooker was the man with whom my father shared a telephone – that was the only way you could get the use of one when they first came to country districts in the early 1920s. On sheep sale days, of course, they'd both want to use the phone, but in spite of my father's generally impatient nature there was never any real trouble over using the line; they'd just wait until it was their turn. Hooker was a forward-thinking man; in the 1920s he imported a German solid-tyred lorry together with heavy Belgian farm horses, which were clumsy but very strong compared to the local horses.

'These characters are all long dead now, but many have children and grandchildren round about. The marsh exerts a strong pull, and those who go away find they miss the place and they often return.'

For Clipping of Sheepe

Clippers are to have 4d a score. Then are you to send them about noon a groates worth of ale and bread and cheese and perhaps a cheesecake and against that time they make an end you are to make ready a dinner for them.

Clippers bring usually two pairs of sheares; you are to give charge to them that they have an especial care of prickinge the skin; wherefore you are to always have a dish standing by either with tar or sheep salve, that if they chance to give a little clippe you may lay tar on it and there is no further danger.

There is 6d allowed to a piper for playing to the clippers all the day.

The Farming and Account Books of Henry Best of Helmswell,
1641

How to Choose a Good Tuppe

Let him be large and well quartered, of a snoode and a good stapple, with a long and bushy tail, without hornes and having both the stones in the codde; and lastly never under two sheare, nor seldom above five for being over young; their blood is hot and the scabbe procured and being over olde their radical moisture is wasted.

The Farming and Account Books of Henry Best of Helmswell,
1641

A Boy at the Plough

WILLIAM WADE

LONGNEWTON, CLEVELAND

*W*illiam Wade's family, on both his mother's and his father's side, had been farmers since at least the early part of the nineteenth century. William was born in 1905 at Plasworth near Chester-le-Street in Country Durham where his grandfather had settled in the middle decades of the nineteenth century after leaving famine-stricken Ireland.

Long Newton Grange sits alone on the top of a raised area of ground which hardly qualifies as a hill, yet gives the farm commanding views of the surrounding countryside. In the distance, smoke from the few remaining industries on Teesside can be seen drifting into the sky some dozen miles away to the east. William came to Long Newton Grange with his father and mother in 1920 when he was thirteen, and although officially still at school he was already part of the farm workforce, as he explained:

'I started working on the farm before I left school, which is what most farmer's sons did. School was all right, but you only needed so much of it if you knew you were going on the land. I was already driving a pair of horses at the plough when I was eleven. As ploughboy to an older, more experienced man you just picked it up; you'd walk by his side, up and down the field or lead the horses now and then, just watching and waiting your turn. And your turn would come but only when the ploughman thought you were ready. He'd start by letting you get the feel of the handles, gradually increasing the length of time you were in charge of the team. If you started to go off the line he was there to set you straight.

'I can remember mowing hay for the army in the Great War. We used a horse for that, too, gradually walking it round the field with the blades off to the side of the mower, which was towed behind; a simple gearing system meant that the cutting blades were turned by the motion of the wheels as the mower was pulled by the horse. I also drove the horses on the waggon that went round to pick up the hay. We were working with soldiers then, who'd been sent to help us; they pitched the hay up to us, while we made sure it was piled up nicely on the waggon.'

William Wade had a rich store of memories of farming during the Great War and the 1920s. In his latter years he was confined to the house by illness but his memory remained sharp. 'I find it sad, looking back all those years, very sad,' he said. 'The idea that it is all over for me now, even though I had a good life. I find it sad even thinking about all the horses I worked with; the fact that they have all gone, too, and everything has changed.'

One of William's six sons had agreed to take over the farm but the others had all helped at various times which meant that it was many years since William had employed anyone from outside. 'We just couldn't afford to, and we didn't need to once modern tractors and equipment came in,' says William. But things were very different when he first began working on the farm:

'Well, the Great War made the biggest difference because suddenly we found that the army was commandeering just about everything – suddenly we farmers were central to the national effort, and the army was taking every cow, every potato and every haystack round about. When they helped themselves to a stack they used to put a pole in it, with WD – for War Department – written on it in big letters, and no one would dare touch it then.

'The soldiers who were sent to work with us were

mostly pretty good, although some had no experience of working on the land. But others were real countrymen, and there were some first-class horsemen among them. On this farm at that time we would have between twelve and fourteen horses at any one time. We used to breed from them, and when the youngsters were old enough they were sold, and went to work either in the towns or down the mines. This might seem cruel, but horses were essential because there was no mechanical means to get the coal back from the face to the shafts, and we all needed coal: everyone did, for fires, heating and industry. Apart from wood, if you were in the country, there was nothing else.

'The small ponies went to the coal mines, and the slightly bigger ones to the ironstone mines at Cleveland. A countryside without horses was inconceivable then; even when the new tractors were being talked about – and you could get them from about 1920, although the early ones were unreliable – no one believed they would ever take over from the horse. Horses were everywhere and used for just about everything: moving people and goods, carting farm produce, drilling, ploughing, harrowing, haymaking – everything.'

William's farm was only a dozen or so miles from what used to be one of Britain's greatest shipbuilding and industrial centres: Teesside. With much of the 1914–18 war effort centred on increasing industrial production, the urban population had to be organised in a way that was previously unheard of. Yet in spite of this, food distribution then, and for many years after, was still locally organised, as William recalled. 'Yes, for many years after we first came here we used to deliver all our produce locally. I remember we used to cart our wheat to a mill at Stockton about eight miles away. We sold twenty tons once, and delivered it in what was called a Rolley, a great heavy four-wheeled waggon that took two tons at a time and needed two horses to pull it. For this work the horses were harnessed one in front of the other, not abreast. Ordinary carts normally carried about a ton, and we would put the corn in sacks which were filled differently for different crops: a sack of wheat always weighed 16 stone, barley 18 stone, beans 22 stone, and so on.'

William had particularly fond memories of farm horses and although, as he admitted, there was an element of sentiment in this, it had a practical side, too: 'Horses were marvellous to work with because they remembered how to do things – you try teaching a tractor anything! If you took your horses the same way each day, or through the same routine, eventually they would virtually work on their own. I enjoyed riding too, and learned when I was four.

'With working horses on a mixed farm like ours we generally got them out to the fields by 7 in the morning. But we'd have been up at 5.30am doing other work before having breakfast at 6.30am. We came back in at midday for our lunch, then back out again till 5pm when we fed the horses and came in for our tea. After tea we'd go and groom the horses, and then it was time for bed.' Work with horses was more time-consuming than directly arduous, although invariably it involved a great deal of walking: 'You always led, drove or walked your horses; they never went at the trot' said William. And the work got slower and harder on heavier soils.

'This is strong clay land; in fact, to be honest, there's too much clay here. It's good land for wheat and grass, but pretty hopeless for crops like potatoes which we've never bothered with much as a result, except during the war when we had to grow them. With a horse we ploughed about an acre a day; with a tractor it's about twenty because you have five furrows on a machine as against one, or at best two, on a horse plough. Mind you, horses and ponies were tough too, and it was nothing to drive a pony twenty-five miles out and twenty-five back in a day.'

Though he had always been a working farmer, William was shrewd enough to buy land whenever he could, and before he retired he had built the farm up to around 840 acres, with 250 sheep and 400 cattle. 'We amalgamated three small farms: Foxhill, Larberry and the oldest, Long Newton Grange, and three of my sons took over the whole lot in partnership.'

A major problem for William until well into the 1940s was the lack of water. There was a well, but in summer it would dry up, and, like many farmers, William had no choice but to hope for regular rainfall. 'We had no river nearby when the well started to get difficult. A water pipe was laid nearby in the early 1940s, but the people who were responsible for it were worried that I'd use too much water so they wouldn't connect me at first, which I thought was a bit unfair.'

The last few Long Newton horses were used for general carting until 1960, which was long after most farmers had got rid of them. 'I liked working with horses because they'd nearly always go without being driven, and knew exactly what they were doing and what you wanted them to do – they only had to do a task a few times to pick it up. Here they used to walk between the stooks of corn, and they'd stop in just the right place without being told so we could lift the hay on to the waggon. A few people still used horses into the 1970s and 1980s, but that was rare. Vaux, the brewery in Sunderland, used horses for local deliveries into the 1970s; horses were and are probably still cheaper than motors for local deliveries.'

The great staple in Durham, as in so many northern counties, was always wool; and if there happened to be a glut of wool at any time the Durham farmers of old didn't rely on modern ideas like intervention buying, they had a far more novel solution, as William remembered: 'Farmers would shear their sheep and if the wool price was too low they'd bury the wool for a year or more! It's hard to believe, I know, and you'd think it would rot, but it never did. Wool is amazing stuff. I'll tell you something else which will show you just how remarkable it is: when the Victorian engineers had to build the main north-south, east coast railway over the Cleveland bog it was always said that they first packed tons of wool into the bog and then ran the rails over that; they knew that wool would make it just as stable as drainage and filling in. It's a true story, and the rail has never been taken up so it still runs over the wool. And in medieval times they used to put wool into a river bed first before laying bridge foundations – oh, yes! it's marvellous stuff!'

On William's traditionally mixed farm, sheep and corn were the mainstay, but, shrewdly, he early on decided that there was also money in milk. 'I started our milk herd: Father didn't like the idea much because he'd never done it, and it was a bit of a step into unknown territory. I remember the first cow we bought cost just £13!'

It wasn't until he was well into his teens that William heard his first wireless, but he can still remember the sense of disbelief as the weak sound crackled over the crystal set. 'It was like magic, you just couldn't believe it. At that time we'd only heard talk of radios, and of course television wasn't even an idea. That set I first heard wasn't even ours, it belonged to one of our farm-workers – the sound was a bit crackly, but it was very exciting. The only other entertainment the modern world had brought us was the cinema, and every now and then we'd traipse off to the pictures in Stockton or Darlington to see the silent films; people would travel miles to see them in those days.'

But farm work being what it is was there was little time for excursions. Every day brought a series of almost endless tasks, for as well as growing crops and rearing animals, farmers had to sell their own produce, as well as buy and sell from each other. 'We used to buy some of our horses from other farmers, perhaps if they had a foal to sell, or we'd go to the regular horse sales at Yarm or at Newcastle. Although we bred our own horses, they were in short supply during the Great War because so many were needed at the front. All we could ever buy in then were horses branded with a "C" on the shoulder, meaning "cast"; in other words they had been rejected by the army perhaps because they were gun shy, or something else made them unsuitable for war.

'The four or five foals we bred each year were sometimes sent to Scotland, to Glasgow where they pulled trams, coal carts and just about everything else. However, horses used to the farm were often terrified by the traffic in the towns and it might take them a while to settle to the work; on at least two occasions I remember horses bolted with me in Stockton – I think they thought they were being chased by a tram!

'Horses can be very funny, too. I had a strange mare, for example, who wouldn't budge for anyone except me and even then I had to feed her a bit of chocolate first!

'For years I rode an old pony to school. The road at the end of the farm track was just a tiny, overgrown, unmetalled lane then, and in fact it stayed like that until just before the Second World War. I used to trot the pony through the snowdrifts in winter unless we were really snowed in, which did happen occasionally. When my sister started going to school we drove together in the pony and trap. It was lovely to trot along the snowy lanes, and when we got to school, which was in the village about two miles away, we'd leave the pony and trap in the pub stables.

'Driving a horse and cart could be very exciting; I remember the first time I took the milk into Stockton it was in a blinding snowstorm. We could hardly see where we were going and there wasn't a soul about – talk about the bleak mid-winter! That would have been about 1925. We got 6d a gallon for the milk then, and you couldn't just take it to one dairy; there were several small ones round

about, and I'd have to take different amounts to each one. Sometimes they wouldn't want any, and if there was a bit of a glut of milk, of course the price would get lower and lower. The dairies could really dictate terms, too – we asked 8d a gallon from one dairy owner, and he said he'd only pay it if the milk reached him every day by 7am. To get it there by then we had to start milking at about 4am; friends said that only two fools like my dad and me would have done it! We stuck it out for a year. All the milking was by hand, then; there was no real skill to it, but some milkers were very fast. We had twelve cows, and it wasn't until about 1942 that we reached forty.

'We had a milking machine by the end of the second war, but still oil lamps in the farmhouse. I thought I'd be clever and try to light the house using some old bus batteries; we were already using them to drive the milk machine, but actually they turned out to be useless for the house so we stuck with the oil lamps until the mid-1950s when the electricity came. Even then they didn't want us to have it, but they needed to lay the cable over my land so I told them if they didn't connect me, they couldn't lay the cable; that soon sorted it out, although the contractor still had to squeeze something out of me – he said he'd connect us if I gave him a goose, but then I thought that was a pretty good bargain!'

One constant revealed through William's memories was the fact that until the 1960s, rural Durham had changed little in centuries. Away from industrial areas, life continued much as it always had done, with little time for entertainment and pleasure in a farming year that demanded almost all the energy a man had. 'It's hard to imagine, now, what it was like round here up to the early 1960s. Just take certain individual things which have vanished, like the local blacksmith. Today the blacksmith is a rarity, but until around 1960 he was one of the most important men in the area; every village, however tiny, had a blacksmith and he would make anything and everything – hinges, bolts, and metal bits of waggons, hooks, and so on.

'Every village and hamlet would also have had a cartwright, or waggon-maker, and styles of waggon would vary between district and even between individual makers. The further afield you went, of course, the greater the difference, which is why we could tell if a passing cart wasn't a local one. For example, Scottish carts were very different from the English ones: the Scottish cart had a lot of iron in it, where the English cart was almost entirely of wood. Irish carts had shafts back and front. The Irish also had special, long, high-sided carts for hay and I remember going to Ireland with my father to buy cattle before the war and seeing fifteen or maybe twenty long Irish hay-carts moving slowly along the road towards Dublin; high up on the hay on every single waggon sat groups of men drinking and playing nap. That was a glorious sight!'

William often went to Ireland in those early days, to buy livestock and to see relatives who were still living there. Though railways and steamers made the longer journeys much easier than they had once been, local transport hadn't advanced much since medieval times. 'Up in the north-east the roads were all unmade until after the second war, and even then a lot of the minor ones were left as tracks. No one really had responsibility for the upkeep of the roads, it was just as it had been centuries before, so we used to try to keep the roads near us as well surfaced as we could by going to collect cinders from a works on Teesside. We'd cart the cinders and then spread them over the potholes and ruts, and this gave the cartwheels something to bite into.

'A fellow who worked for us used to take the horse and cart and go for the cinders regularly. After he'd been going for quite some time I decided I'd do it instead. First time out I'd got halfway to the place where we used to collect the cinders when the horse turned into a pub yard. Horses remember these things, you see, so I knew what the previous fellow had been doing!

'Every pub in the land had stables then, because everyone arrived by cart or on horseback. On market days in the town you often couldn't find a stall for a horse, the place was so packed with carts and ponies, horses and dogs and other livestock. It's a sight few can remember now, and it will never be seen again.

'Quite a few working horses were still helping on the farms well into the 1950s and 1960s in this area; you'd see them along the roads, although they became rarer almost by the day. And even farmers who loved to have them about, found that when the old ones died there was really no point in replacing them; and in many cases you couldn't even if you wanted to, because the farm-horse sales had gone.

'The horse fairs were great fun. I remember once going to Yarm Horse Fair, which was always held in September, to get a pony to run the milk. I found one I liked, and asked the man holding it what he wanted for it; £40 he said, so I offered £30 and we settled on £35. That horse ran the milk every day for seven years; it also worked the horse-driven binder for us at haymaking time, along with two other horses. They were harnessed three abreast, and we always put the weakest horse on the outside; the first or inside horse was called master because he controlled the turn.

'I must have trained hundreds of horses in my time. The best policy was to let them be until they were two years old, or perhaps three; they were allowed to run at grass all that time. We usually started to train a young horse sometime around Christmas. I don't know why then, exactly, but that was usually the time. You got the horse used to being handled, and then put a bridle on it. When it was used to that, you harnessed it in the middle of three horses harnessed abreast, putting it between two old, quiet, experienced horses. At first a young horse was kept in harness for only half a day at a time because it would get sore shoulders if you didn't take things slowly and gradually. It was also important to make sure you had a good, well-fitting collar, and there was a real skill to making a good collar that wouldn't rub. We went to the local saddler for that: he made just about everything and anything to do with leather, and he would always make a one-off if, for example, you had a horse with an odd-shaped neck. He'd also make you a pair of boots if you asked him. One saddler from the old days carried on long after horses disappeared. He was Mr Sample from Great Smeaton; he adapted his business and made saddles and bridles for riding ponies and horses.

'In the old days, farm horses were fed on a mixture of hay, oats, flaked maize and crushed beans, and if a horse was well treated it might work for up to twenty years. In the north when a mare foaled we'd leave the foal in a farm building during the day and put the mare to grass till lunchtime. She'd then be put with the foal for a while, then put out again till evening. That's the way we did it, though I know that in the south the foal went to the fields with the mare.

'For ploughing we had only two instructions for the horses: we'd shout "haa" if we wanted the horse to turn right, and "gee back" if we wanted it to turn left. Horses were harnessed abreast for ploughing in many areas, but here I often ploughed with a team of three in line; the quickest was always put at the front and the strongest at the back or in the heel position, because turning at the headlands relied on the back horse and it was hard work for her.

'A horse-drawn plough is difficult to control at first because it must cut in a straight line and to an even depth; this isn't easy, because while you concentrate on these things you also have to concentrate on three great horses. We used a wheeled plough which was easier, but my father, who was a champion ploughman in his time, used a most difficult plough which had no wheels at all. He once took the wheels off my plough and I got in a right mess! The wheels made it easier because with the big wheel in the furrow and the small wheel on the land, the top of the furrow, the whole thing naturally tended to stay on an even keel. Without wheels the plough slipped up and down and from side to side unless you really knew what you were doing.

'Ransome, Simms and Geoffrey were famous plough-makers, and they used to employ my father to plough with their equipment; he did it so well that it was a good advertisement for their tackle. In return, when the ploughshare wore out, or any other part, my father was always given a new part by the company for nothing. All the metal parts of the plough were of locally made iron and very strong, cast by Teesdale Bros who had a foundry nearby. They made everything – ploughshares, drills, scufflers, everything.

'All the time I was growing up we kept the cattle chained in their stalls and every cow was fed individually. Leaving the cattle in the fields is a recent thing. You had to feed individually because different cows needed different amounts if you were to get the maximum yield of milk from them. I started with Shorthorns; they were red, white or a mix of the two colours, or sometimes roan. Then in 1932 we went over to Ayrshires because they'd been tested for tuberculosis. My sons changed to half Ayrshires and half Friesians.

'I started with 135 acres in Father's time. He added 214 acres and we were always adding odd little pieces to that.'

Amid the tales of increasing prosperity, William acknowledged that, like most farmers, he'd had his ups and downs; inevitably the 1930s were as bad in the northeast as anywhere. 'Things were dreadful in the 1930s, which is probably why the government and the Europeans don't want to go back to the sort of free market for farm produce we had then. At that time the free market meant thousands of farmers going out of business. During those days the only way we could make a living was by buying Irish cattle, fattening them, and selling them on, and even that didn't always work. I remember one year we bought thirty Galloway bullocks and fed them all winter. We'd paid £14 per head for them, and after feeding them for months we got only £20 each for them. It just wasn't worth doing.

'The second war really got farming out of the doldrums because suddenly everyone needed us and all the food we could produce; and that might also explain why, after the war, there was another slump.'

The economics of farming have always been difficult or controversial, but whether their standard of living is high or low there seems to be a lasting commitment to the land among most farmers that overrides temporary economic realities. This attachment to the land undoubtedly contains an element of sentiment, which is presumably why so many farmers refuse to pack up and do something else during difficult periods; there is an idea that somehow farmers are born to that way of life, however hard it may be. Most of William Wade's memories were of difficult times, but it was impossible to imagine him doing anything else; it was almost as if the harshness of life on the land was a part of what made it so compelling, as William recalled

'I remember, for example, bringing about thirty cattle from the railway station twenty miles away. We'd bought them in Ireland and I had the dog to help me, but twenty miles along rough roads is a long way to drive that many cattle in a day. By the time we'd got halfway back to the farm the dog's pads were worn away and its feet were bleeding, so I had to put it over my shoulders and carry it.

'Farming could be a cruel business in those days

too, and particularly, I think, in Ireland. For example, I remember de-horning hundreds of cattle without using an anaesthetic as you would have to now. There was blood absolutely everywhere and the cows were obviously in pain; we just sawed the horns off, and if you looked down the stump you could see into their skulls. It was terrible, but we knew no better then. If you left their horns to grow on they could do a lot of damage to each other and to you. We had one lovely old cow called Ghandi, and she was such a nice old thing we couldn't bring ourselves to cut her horns off; but being among a lot of cattle without horns she quickly realised that she could dominate them all, and became a terrible bully.

'I think the funniest thing I remember from my long farming years was the time I drove a flock of sheep into Stockton town centre. Driving sheep through big towns was an everyday occurrence in the 1920s and 1930s because there were no lorries and no other way to move them. Usually it went all right and the sheep stayed close together, but on this occasion for some unaccountable reason one of my sheep jumped straight through the plate-glass window of a shop. The sheep was all right, but the shopkeeper wasn't amused!'

Starting Young

As a babe the first words he lisps are the names of the
horses. Does he cry – he is taken to see Prince, or lifted
up to pat Diamond. He no sooner learns to walk than
he finds his way to the stables, toddling with the rest
of the family after da da as he spends hour after hour
baiting his charges.

Thus from earliest infancy he is receiving a technical
education. He hears of nothing, thinks of nothing, but
of that one business by which he is to live; the stable
becomes playroom and schoolroom combined; all his
ideas centre in it and gather round it and when in due
course he becomes a mate, he displays at once an inborn
and inbred faculty for managing horses.

Richard Heath, *The English Peasant*, 1893

Falling Prices

At Chertsey where we came into Surrey again, there
was a fair for horses, cattle and pigs. I did not see any
sheep. Everything was exceedingly dull. Cart colts, two
and three years old, were selling for less than a third of
what they sold for in 1813.

The cattle were of an inferior description to be sure;
but the price was low almost beyond belief. Cows,
which would have sold for 15 shillings in 1813 did
not get buyers at 3 shillings. I had not time to enquire
about the pigs, but a man told me that they were cheap.

William Cobbett, *Rural Rides*, 1830

DICK ROWLEY WILLIAMS
DENBIGH, NORTH WALES

*B*lundell Edward Rowley Williams might easily have been described as a gentleman farmer. But if this is taken to mean a farmer who simply gets others to do the work for him, then it will not do at all. For Dick Rowley Williams was a man who liked to get his hands dirty, and as well as indulging his lifelong enthusiasm for the pursuit of foxes, he kept his remote Welsh farm going for seventy years through his own resources and hard work. Glyn Arthur is a lovely Regency house built by an ancestor of Dick's, the family having owned the farm since the eighteenth century; it stands alone high on the Denbigh hills with glorious views of the town of Denbigh in the distance.

'Six generations of my family have now lived and worked here,' said Dick proudly. A quiet man who smiled readily and displayed the formal good manners of a vanished era, he was proud of his family's long association with Wales generally, and with Glyn Arthur in particular. 'My great-great-grandfather built the place using stone from a local quarry. We think work started on the house we see now in 1790, and it was certainly finished by 1800; but the old part of the house, to which my great-great-grandfather's house was "tacked on", as it were, has been here since about 1600. He could afford to build a new house simply because he had the good sense to marry an heiress. We haven't always been quite so sensible since!'

Dick took an active interest in the farm until he was well into his nineties. Farming seemed to be bred in his family, although the different generations approached it in markedly different ways. 'I suppose it was inevitable that I would be interested in farming, having been born here among farming people and where all the talk was of farming. But my own father was a gentleman farmer in the sense that he had a private income and so didn't worry too much if the farm itself didn't make any money.

'I was born in 1903, and my earliest memories are of riding various ponies. I always loved horses and ponies and looking back now I seem to have spent my whole childhood on horseback. I rode from the time I was a very small boy; in fact it was unthinkable then for a boy, or indeed a girl, not to learn to ride – it was how we got about, and of course you couldn't hunt if you didn't ride, and all our friends and neighbours hunted. Hunting lay at the heart of all our social activities. I was perhaps three or four years old when I learned to ride, and I was still riding in my seventies. I was joint-master of the Flint and Denbigh hounds for more than fifty years, and my son is now joint-master; so hunting, like farming, is very much in the family. I was very keen on hunting from an early age, it was just so exciting, but of course when I was sent away to school at Shrewsbury I couldn't do much of hunting or anything else for that matter.'

After Shrewsbury, farming wasn't an automatic choice for a young man with good connections and a good education, and like many well-off country families, the Rowley Williamses decided that their son would benefit from spending some time abroad. 'When I left school I was sent to Rhodesia, largely I think because no one had the faintest idea what to do with me! I worked on a remote farm owned by a friend of the family, and all I remember is that after clearing the scrub using oxen, we grew tobacco and maize. I was also sent to France for a while to learn to speak the language. If you were brought up as a gentleman in the early part of the twentieth century these were things you needed. I suppose I could have gone into business and made a lot of money; but even then I dreaded the idea of working for someone else on a sort of five-days-a-week, nine-to-five basis.'

For Dick, the attractions of making money were as nothing to the attractions of hunting and shooting. 'Yes, I might have made more money if I'd done that sort of thing, but I realised pretty early on that I would be far happier farming, even if it meant making no money at all. The fact that I loved country life and everything it entailed also came into the decision, of course. If I were asked to sum up my life, I'd say that I didn't make much money but I enjoyed myself.

'I was also very keen on training and working sheepdogs. I never did this to win competitions, but simply because I enjoyed it – sheepdogs, and breeding and schooling horses. However, from an early age I worked on the farm, although we did employ farmworkers. I had to help with the horses, and with the sheep; in fact with just about everything, at one time or another.

'When I was a young man, shearing sheep was a far more exhausting and difficult business than it is now because it was all done with hand shears or clippers. They were a bit like a big pair of iron scissors. A good man might shear forty sheep in a day, whereas nowadays a good man with electric shears will do three hundred sheep in the same time. With hand shears, before you could do anything you had to lift each sheep onto a special bench and then tie its legs. It was a laborious business.'

Glyn Arthur had always been a remote farm, and it changed little over Dick's long lifetime. The only difference between isolation at the turn of the twentieth century and isolation in more recent years was that the spell is more easily and perhaps more comfortably broken. The narrow mountainous roads are no longer made from pounded stones, and in a car, the town is only ten minutes away. However, the Rowley Williamses were always able to travel in some style – long before cars were thought of the family had their own phaetons and broughams, gentlemen's carriages whose names are now quite unfamiliar to the vast majority of the population.

'Yes, when I was a boy we had a number of different kinds of carriage. The phaeton, I recall, was a rather grand thing. It had four wheels – unlike the dog-cart or the gamboge which had two – and was pulled by two fine horses. It was a very comfortable, sprung affair which would easily carry four people in great style and comfort. The dog-cart could also carry four. It had two seats in front, and the underlings – the groom or the children – sat on a sort of box at the back; below this was a board on which you rested your feet. None of the roads was metalled then, as you can imagine, and we were often cut off – we are still often cut off in winter by drifting snow; and when the valley flooded even the carriages were hopeless, so when I was a young man we used to go by sailing boat to Denbigh to the hunt balls.'

The Rowley Williamses were always quite happy to go for weeks without visiting the town; and several generations had always lived happily in the house together, making their own amusements. Towards the end of Dick's life he shared the house with his wife as well as their son and daughter-in-law and four children. 'Long after the electricity came we still had to resort to lamps and candles in winter when something went wrong, and although we were isolated here there was always plenty to do; we had lots of friends to go and see, we visited each other's houses, as we still do, and there was hill hunting, tennis and rough shooting. And of course as a child one could be mischievous and invent one's own pastimes. I used to get up to lots of pranks. I remember once as the maid was serving us at dinner – the whole family had sat down – I produced a live slow-worm out of my pocket, and a great pile of plates crashed to the ground from the maid's hands. I was reprimanded rather severely for that!

'In my youth it was still the custom in many, if not most country houses, to say morning prayers in the house. The head of the household, one's father, would lead the prayers. One morning during prayers I found it difficult to take it seriously because I had noticed that our terrier was taking a great interest in a big old cupboard in the corner of the room, what we called a Jonah cupboard. As soon as I could I opened the cupboard door and spotted a big rat. I prodded him, he leapt out and our terrier caught him in mid-air. That, I'm afraid, was of far more interest to me than the prayers on which I should have been concentrating! I suppose like all children I used to do some pretty mad things; I was terribly fond of chickens, I remember, but I couldn't afford any of the fancy poultry which I loved, so I used to buy ordinary chickens and paint their legs bright colours! However, even while I was very young I was helping out around the farm and learning the ropes in a more serious way.'

As farm incomes dropped and the family money began to diminish, the days of farming in what might best be termed a rather amateur if gentlemanly fashion had to come to an end, and Dick soon found that farm work had become a full-time business. 'I used to get up at five and ride down to help with the milking, which of course was all by hand; then I'd help feed the pigs. Our pigs weren't like modern pigs, they were damn great things that used to attack me when I went in to them! During haymaking time we worked from dawn to dusk for seven shillings and sixpence a week, and at lambing time we'd be up half the night wandering the fields.'

Although they have lived in Wales for generations, the Rowley Williamses sounded thoroughly English, and their outlook was far more cosmopolitan than that of other local people who rarely left the area even for a few weeks. In fact isolation and insularity inevitably produced a certain amount of eccentricity among the local population, as Dick remembers: 'Our blacksmith, for example, was a rather strange chap. I remember chatting to him one day and telling him that he ought to get married. He said in his lovely Welsh accent "Ah, but you don't know what you're getting, do you, when you get married." All right, I said, get a housekeeper then. "Oh, but I'll have to pay her, won't I?" he said. I thought that was terribly funny.'

On a hill farm where every bit of grass was needed, the rabbit was considered a serious pest, particularly as the species seemed to be most prolific in Britain just at the time when farm incomes were at their lowest, in the thirties and forties. So when myxomatosis came in the 1950s the family welcomed the rapid and almost complete disappearance of the rabbit population, and Dick was still grateful that myxy did what no amount of shooting and gassing could ever have managed. 'We reckoned that four rabbits would eat as much as a sheep, so we were very glad when myxomatosis came in and virtually wiped them out. It was particularly important for us because on a hill farm it's a constant struggle to make ends meet. When I first really got to grips with the land here it was during the Second World War. I had been a captain in the Royal Welch Fusiliers but I was released because they thought I would do more for the war effort on a farm than in uniform.

'We knew that in spite of the hilly country we had quite good soil, so we tried to eradicate the bracken; and although people said it could never be done, and that even if we could do it, we'd never be able to plough and harrow the steep hillsides, we thought we'd have a go. And we did it. I'd done similar work in Rhodesia so I hired a tractor with caterpillar tracks and used a horse-drawn plough on the really steep bits.'

Dick's greatest moment on the farm undoubtedly came when he created useful land out of what had been bracken-covered hillside, and the story of how he did it made him something of a celebrity, whose activities were described in glowing detail in local newspapers in the 1940s. But of course the incentive was there, because for the first time since the Great War the nation needed as much food as it could produce itself; and suddenly, after the long years of agricultural depression, the farmer was a very important man indeed. After one particular feature in a local paper Dick became known as the 'man who cultivated a mountain'.

'Farming was at its worst in the 1930s and 1940s. You had to accept that one year you made a bit of money, and the next you made none. We schooled and sold horses when things were very bad, but farm wages were minute then – thirty bob [shillings] and a cottage was what we paid for a farm worker. And you could buy a sheep then for thirty bob, though a cow might cost £20.

'I was a farming adviser during the Second War, partly because we'd done well here in difficult circumstances and so they thought I might be able to help others in similar circumstances. But farmers were opinionated old-so-and-sos then as now, and they didn't always take kindly to my advice. Bad reactions to a visit never went beyond rudeness and bad temper with me, but we knew of other advisers who were threatened with guns. Mostly we just asked them to upgrade their cattle and improve their land; and remember, this was a time when we were all being asked to dig for victory, so it was important work.

'As ours was predominantly a sheep area, one of my jobs was to assess a farmer's rams. If the ram was good enough I'd put a mark on it; if it wasn't, I'd suggest to the farmer that he get another. One chap I talked to about this had already threatened an official with his gun, but I found I got on all right with him. I told him he needed a new ram, and he just said "You give me one, then". So I told him he could have any ram of mine he liked, and that seemed to do the trick.

'Like all farmers before the last war, we walked all our animals to market along the roads. To get to Denbigh with twenty or thirty sheep would take about two and a half hours, but many times we'd drive the sheep there, fail to sell them and have to drive them all the way back again! And with geese on the old drovers' roads, we'd dab their feet in pitch before we set off so they wouldn't wear raw and bleed on the stony track.

'Farm incomes improved dramatically after the second war, and in 1959 I bought another farm some miles away for £10,000. That was a lot of money then, but I sold it thirty years later for £300,000, so I didn't do too badly!

'On a farm you never know what you may have to do – I remember my wife coming back from a hunt ball in a rather lovely dress and then, still in the same dress, having to help with a sow that had got into the wrong pen. We had about thirty sows then, but we never really made any money with them.

'We had a car quite early on, an old Austin that lasted for twenty-three years. Then we had a Morris 8, but we had to get rid of that because the nanny got too fat to fit in it! In the days before the motor car we thought nothing of travelling long distances by carriage. The dog cart could seat four comfortably, and we might go twenty miles in it; and when my father stopped riding to hounds he used a carriage instead, and raced about the fields in that. He always managed to keep up with the field, and must have covered as many as forty miles in it in a day.

'My mother always hunted, and rode side saddle which has virtually died out now; she was a marvellous horsewoman. She would always go to and from the meet in the carriage with the horse tied behind; but I often hacked ten miles to a meet and then ten miles back at the end of a long day's hunting. People thought nothing of such distances in those days. By the 1970s our hunting country had been badly cut up by roads and that is only likely to get worse.

'In the 1920s you might have paid £30–£50 for a good horse – a working horse, that is – and it would probably keep going until it was twenty. We'd usually give it lighter duties then. I remember we had two Suffolk Punches, one of which ran away with me one day; it just made a dash for the road with me hanging on to the harness. I stopped it after a few hundred yards, but by then we were virtually wedged in the hedge!

'We had six men with six horses as well as a land girl and my wife, and we all worked full time, but it was still slow going. What we called the teamsman looked after the horses, but at harvest-time all our friends would come to help and we could all turn our hands to just about anything round the farm. We used to cut the hay, give it two days to dry, and then turn it with a horse-drawn turner, a clever mechanical thing which would just flip the hay over as it lay scattered about the field. When both sides were dry we cocked it, which basically meant we piled it up in little heaps. We used tripods for some years, which helped the hay to dry more quickly; as the name suggests, the tripod was a three-legged device designed to keep the air circulating under each pile of hay, and they worked very well indeed. We always called our haystack the Queen Mary, simply because it was so enormous. Even in the early days we were rather modern here, and one of the things we had was a hoist for the hay which was operated by a horse. Before we built our Queen Mary we'd cover the floor with brushwood first to keep the hay above the damp.

'Hay-carrying waggons were built specifically for that one task, having flat bottoms and very high sides. Even so, the hay would be loaded until it was so high that it could become unstable if you didn't know what you were doing.

I remember once I was right at the top of a full haycart when the lead horse turned too quickly and I came off – I was lucky not to be injured. Farms are dangerous places, or they can be. On another occasion I got pushed right into a thick thorn hedge by a bull. I was in my suit as I'd just got back from town, when I found that our bull had got out of the field he shared with some heifers. I prodded him with a pickel, a small pitchfork, to encourage him to go back in through the gate, but he turned and chased me. I almost made it to the gate by the road, but not quite, and he hit me in the chest and ripped a great hole in my smart jacket. I was all right, but I was furious about my suit so I turned and shouted at him and waved my arms. I was so cross it worked and he turned and fled! But I must have looked very funny running across that field in my suit with my two dogs and a bull right behind me!

'In total I followed hounds from the age of six until the age of seventy-six, which may be some kind of record. I hunted with several packs. I had many falls, but few nasty ones. Once I went down with a horse that rolled on me, and had such a terrible bruise on my face that I couldn't shave for a week; it made my neck very bad too, so I went to an osteopath, but I think his treatment was worse than the injury – I thought he was going to wring my neck! Another time I was brought down by a pheasant, of all things, which flew through the horse's legs and made it stumble and down we went.

'Towards the end of my time we had just under one thousand sheep, and they grazed our 380 acres as well as a sheep walk that we rented. We still had one farm-worker, but we couldn't have afforded more and even if we'd had the money there'd be little for them to do because mechanisation and electricity and machines made everything so much easier. We used to have a cook, two maids and a nanny, but those days are long gone. The nanny, who lived in, was paid £16 a year.

'The only labour-saving device we had in my youth was a waterwheel. It was set up on the stream to drive our wood saw and to grind our corn. You just pulled up a sluice, the water came through, hit the wheel and you were in business.'

Like many country houses, Glyn Arthur had an inside loo by the end of the nineteenth century but it was reserved strictly for use by the women of the house; the men still had to go outside, and they continued to do so well into the twentieth century. The staff had another, entirely separate loo, which was also outside. Dick laughed at how different things were in his youth; but he was proud that, however much things had changed, the presence of another generation of his family in the house was assured. He had four children: Peter, who took over the farm; Richard, Elizabeth and Edmund.

One characteristic of the Rowley Williamses that non-hunting people find curious is that, like most country people who loved hunting they were very fond of the fox, and over the years kept several as pets. 'We had one for a number of years when I was young, and if I shouted "Come on, Charlie!" he would rush over and jump into my arms. However, every fox will wander away eventually; I think the mating and travelling urge is just too strong and eventually they just have to go.

'Other foxes we kept used to wander around the house and sleep with the dogs. One used to play with the hounds – the fox would hide in the shrubbery in the garden while the hound puppies tried to find it. They'd draw for him in the undergrowth while he sat, with a rather superior look on his face, bang in the middle of the lawn!'

Dick confessed that, great though his love of farming is, he does occasionally regret that he did not devote more time to his other great love: art. From a dusty cupboard he revealed an ancient sketchbook filled with exquisite pictures of horses and ponies, sheep and other animals, landscapes and the hills of his beloved Wales. 'Yes, I studied art for a while in the 1930s, because I found I was quite good at it; but the farm was so busy that I did little over the years before Peter began to take over. But I have this book of drawings, and several of my pictures are framed on the walls here in the house, so there will at least be something of my artistic side when I'm gone.'

For Loading Hay

About the time that we begin to cut grass we send word to the wright to come and see that the axle trees and felfes of the waines be sound and firm. We load constantly in hay time with two or three waines. The usual manner is to send out with each wain three folkes viz two men and a woman, whereof the one of the men is a loader, the other the forker and the woman to rake after the wain.

Loaders are to be forewarned that they make their loades broad and large, but not over high for fear of throwing over. A stack is always made after the manner of a long square; having a ridge like the ridge of a house.

The Farming and Account Books of Henry Best of Helmswell,
1641

The Field

I am Barter's now, last year for Gatehouse I, Nurtured a pretty crop of rye, When Barter's dead, some new-named man will say, 'All this is mine,' and go the deathward way.

Rye, vetch and man, all to the seasons yield, While I lie low, the same old smiling field.

Anon

Worthless Fellows

Farmers are often I think worthless fellows. Few lords will cheat and when they do they will be ashamed of it; farmers cheat and are not in the least ashamed. They have all the sensuous vices roo of the nobility, with cheating into the bargain.

Boswell's Life of Samuel Johnson, 1790

AT THE HIRING FAIR

JOHN ELGEY

GREAT DRIFFIELD, HUMBERSIDE

' *A* working farm in the 1930s was always busy with men: men working in the fields and around the yards, men looking after the animals, and men clearing the ditches or cutting the hedges.'

John Elgey was a tall, straight-backed Yorkshireman who flatly refused to accept the local government reorganisation of the 1970s that removed official recognition from the East Riding of Yorkshire where he had always lived. Though he never married – 'the right girl never came along' he said with a wink – it was only in his latter years that the farm suffered any lack of company. 'Normally we had twelve men living and working here at any one time' he remembered. 'Most of them were taken on from the hiring fairs, held all over the country in the market towns usually in November; those men wanting to be hired would walk around slowly, perhaps with a bit of straw sticking out of a pocket or in a lapel. It's only now that the days of the hiring fair are gone that I realise what an ancient and in many ways strange practice it was.'

John Elgey was born in 1914 in the big eighteenth-century house where his nephew was eventually to succeed him. In his final years John retired to what was once the stockman's house. This was at the side of a farmyard littered with implements from the past: old horse ploughs of different sorts lay where they were left when the horses finally disappeared for good; wrought-iron drills made by the local blacksmith and designed to be pulled by horses leant against the mellow brick, half-hidden among the wild flowers. Farming in the East Riding had been John's life's work, and through his own long life and through the lives of the men and women he knew as a young man, he became a great chronicler of the farming past. He also owned a large collection of old farming implements, including dozens of curious picks, rakes, forks and shovels, each with its own highly specialised function. John had seen and experienced at first hand all the changes farming experienced in the twentieth century; and through family stories passed down via his grandparents he was a mine of information on how farming had changed in the nineteenth century.

'My grandfather first took the lease on this farm in 1908 and my earliest memories are all of horses; horses did everything, and the work was hard but healthy. We always had about fourteen working horses here, largely Shires and Clydesdales; and as well as the adult horses we would also have as many as ten non-working youngsters, horses that were growing up ready to take the place of their parents when they were no longer able to work. We bred our own horses, and in fact the situation with horses was just like it is with farmers, one generation taking over from the next.

'Until the Great War the horsemen started work at six in the morning and didn't finish till six at night. After the war the men started at seven and worked till half-past five, which was easier on them. But in this part of the world you didn't stop at midday, you worked right through!'

John left school in 1930 when he was sixteen, and went to Worksop College which was a boarding school. 'I was there for five long years, during which time I saw home only during the holidays,' he said with a note of regret. 'I used to take the train from the village down the road. In fact the railway used to run across the farm, until the cuts in the 1960s. We had our own little station, but virtually all the traffic to and from the station was horse-drawn, at least until the end of the 1920s. A few of the better-off farmers had cars, but actually they were almost as slow as the horses anyway; they trundled along the roads at fifteen or twenty miles an hour, and it was a real treat for the village children to see them. No one thought of driving tests in those days, either – I've never passed a test and I've driven for sixty-two years without an accident!

'The system with the horses here on this farm was fairly simple. The head horseman, or waggoner, had his own stable, by which I mean he was completely in control of it – he had six horses and what was called a waggoner's lad, his assistant really. Under the waggoner's lad was the third lad (there was no second lad for some reason), then came the fourth lad, and sometimes what we called the little lad or box lad.

'It was quite a team, but the horses had to be looked after properly because they ran the farm. The waggoner supervised all those under him, and above the waggoner was the farm foreman. The farmworkers might include two or three married men from the village who walked up to us every day, or we'd hire single men at the hiring fair. The hiring fair in November, in Martinmas week to be precise, was at Driffield, and there we'd hire men for a year with the stipulation that they could have one week off. Not very generous I know by today's standards, but it was the way all farmers did it then.'

A gentle man, quietly spoken and often smiling, John had few romantic illusions about the past, though at the same time he refused to dismiss all the old ideas as outmoded and useless. 'I do think one good thing we were given as youngsters was responsibility. For example, I was still in my teens when Dad first sent me to the hiring fair. I was extremely nervous, but I knew I had to do it. When I got there I wandered around for a while knowing what to do in theory, but unable to carry it out in practice. Then I plucked up the courage and walked across to the next two men I saw; I told them where I was from, and asked if they wanted work. I suppose I had just assumed they'd say yes, and couldn't believe my ears when they turned me down flat. The usual reason – and it was one I was given on this occasion – was that "they didn't want to go our way". Sometimes they'd say no because a particular farmer had a reputation as a bad master.

'The workmen would always ask "Is it a good meat house?"; meaning, would they get plenty to eat. Some would want to know how much salmon they would have to eat, which was a serious question because farms on estates where there were salmon rivers were often fed on fish from the river every day for weeks through the summer, and they didn't like it. Or up towards Whitby they'd worry that the farmer would give them sea fish every day because it was cheaper than meat.'

John explained that men at the hiring fair were almost always taken on for a full year; it meant that if they left after six months they weren't paid a penny. They received their full wages only at the end of the year, which may seem hard by today's standards, but, again, it was a system handed down from time immemorial. 'That was the way it had been done for longer than anyone could remember, and in those days people didn't dare to deviate from the way things were supposed to be done.'

However, what may sound like a kind of slavery in

theory often worked rather well in practice, since the farmworker would have little time for leisure, and he could be sure of a roof over his head as well as board and lodging for the whole period of his year-long contract with the farmer. 'Some men were quite happy where they worked; our foreman and his wife, for example, stayed with us for thirty-seven years and the wife used to cook for the men. All twelve used to sleep in one big bedroom which we called the dormitory, with two men to a bed; the foreman's wife made the beds every day. It all seems like another world now, but that's the way it was.'

John's collections of old farm implements included a tiny child's hayfork, and a wide, beautifully polished grain shovel especially made to avoid bruising the corn. A few well-made pieces of heavy oak furniture around his sitting-room had been handed down through succeeding generations of his family. John explained how the farming year was organised when he was a young man in the 1920s:

'It was pretty straightforward. You tried to get all your wheat sown by Martinmas, that is, by November, and then you carried on ploughing through the winter so there was land ready to be sown with barley and oats in the spring. The weather had to be pretty atrocious for you not to get out in the fields because the work had to be done in time; you just got wet, but with a thick wool coat and a sack over you, you didn't get too cold, and anyway you were working too hard to get cold!

'Our plough teams consisted of two horses and a plough with a single furrow eight or nine inches wide. The ploughman always had a boy with him, and the head ploughman always started up the field with the others setting off behind him and to the side following his line. Boys following learned how to plough simply by watching the ploughman. A boy might start at twelve years old and take a plough at thirteen or perhaps fourteen, but by then if he was destined to be a ploughman he would already have learned a lot during his holidays from school and in his spare time. Though the ploughman's life was hard, a ploughman's son wouldn't be wanting to stay at school rather than going on the land: he'd be itching to follow his father. I suppose as with all children it was simply a question of wanting to be grown up.

'It's fairly simple to plough across the field, but on the headland the plough could easily tip over because you didn't have an existing furrow to keep the thing even, and of course it was very tiring to get it good and straight and even unless you really knew what you were doing. That's where the real skill came in. Up on the headland you let it run on the heel of the plough and on the long-shanked wheel. After your first mark across the field you came back on yourself and it was easier, but drawing that first furrow was a real skill. We called it a rig, that is, the furrows and the high ground on the land. These days the reversible plough doesn't leave ridges and furrows as the old ploughs used to, and of course it's much quicker. With horses, the speed depended a lot on how fit the horses were and on the skill of the ploughman. Of course if the ploughman was particularly good and keen at his work, things went very well.'

'Unlike many farms Neswick still had farm-workers, but where there were once twelve men in John's latter days there were only two; with the aid of modern technology, two men were far more productive than twelve used to be.

'The average yield of corn and wheat in the twenties and thirties was one ton per acre; today it's more like three tons per acre, but farmers are not cleverer, or more skilful, it's just that the scientists have moved in. We have all sorts of wonder chemicals today, and the plant breeders give us strains of wheat and grass that the bugs don't like. And diseases and weeds that once would have devastated a crop can now be controlled easily; for example in the old days the men would have had to dig out the thistles from a field of wheat by hand.

'On the bigger farms owned by the gentlemen, the farmer himself hardly got involved at all with the day-to-day running of the farm, whereas on a smaller place like this you might have to help with anything and everything. It was all a bit vague, though; my father would just give the foreman a rough idea of what was needed each day, and then the foreman would organise the men to get it done. But Father would go to market once a week and do all the buying and selling. When I started on the farm it used to annoy me that he disappeared to market like this every week, but then he didn't really need to be around all the time as long as I was here along with the men.

'Officially my father took over the tenancy from my grandfather in 1915, but for all practical purposes a neighbouring farmer ran the place during those first few years because Dad was away at the war until 1918. He was lucky: he came back and hadn't been wounded, though he'd suffered badly from trench fever. I remember him soon after the war always riding a horse around the farm, something he loved to do.

'He was also a bit absent-minded – we kept a lot of sheep then, and once he went to see the shepherd when the sheep were in the turnip field; they talked for a while about this and that, then Dad wandered off home, forgetting all about the horse and leaving it standing in the field! He was very forgetful.

'I learned to ride when I was very young – you weren't properly educated if you couldn't ride well in those days – and I kept at it until the start of the second war. When I was nine I used to go on my pony to be taught by the parson in a village four miles away; since all the other children went to school by pony too, I was quite happy with the arrangement. Then my sister started school, and as we had only the one pony, we put it in a little trap and the gardener drove us both to school; we had to walk back in the evening, although the gardener sometimes met us with the trap. A bit later we got bicycles, and that was a real treat because they were all the rage then, with more and more people buying them. They gave you such independence, and all on roads where there was no danger from traffic – because there wasn't any – and no fear of being attacked by a madman or sex maniac. It just never seemed to happen in those days.

'When I went to school on my pony I suppose that in the four miles I had to travel I might see two or three big carrying waggons, or perhaps the butcher and the baker making their rounds in their specially made, horse-drawn vans with their name and the nature of their trade emblazoned on the side. All the farms and houses had their bread and meat delivered; in the first place it was the best way for the tradesman to make a sale, and better for him than to wait until we came to him because this wouldn't be often – a trip into town was a big event for us, and took a lot of organising. So the butcher came to us twice a week; with twelve men and the family to feed we got through a lot of meat. And of course there was no electricity, and so no fridges or any way to store food for long. Thus the meat arrived and we ate it within a day or two.

Although there was no television or radio, my three brothers, two sisters and I were never bored. We played the sort of games that are still played, like snakes and ladders and draughts; though with the increasing popularity of computer games I wonder how much longer they will last. The girls learned to sew and cook very early in life because it was expected that they would marry and do all these things for their husbands; by the time they were twelve they could make dresses and cook all sorts of things. Nowadays girls aren't taught anything in that line at all.'

Neswick Farm was well off the beaten track, and because the oil lamps that lit the house were not terribly efficient – 'they cast a poor yellow light and made shadows everywhere,' said John – the family made several attempts to find a better, do-it-yourself system. 'We rigged up acetylene gas lamps. These lamps were fitted to the walls of the rooms, and had lead pipe running from them, back to an old outhouse where we kept a special generator. You had to fill this with carbide which came in big drums, in the form of what looked like big stones. You put the carbide – the stones – into a trough, which then slid into a big tube in the generator; then you carefully screwed home a gas-tight door. Then you set the thing going: water dripped onto the carbide inside the generator which caused the gas to come off; the vessel in which the gas was released was like a barrel floating in a bigger barrel of water, and as the gas built up, the floating barrel rose higher in the water, then as you used up the gas it gradually sank. When it had all gone the lights went out and you started all over again – unless it was in the middle of one of Mother's parties, when we'd get out the old paraffin lamps.

'It wasn't until after the second war that we finally got mains water and electricity, and we only got it then because of the army. There were troops in a big house near here; they'd commandeered it, and of course they had water and electricity piped up to them. When the soldiers left for Dunkirk we tapped into the pipes that had supplied them; otherwise I think we would have waited much longer.

'The waggons we used here were four-wheeled Yorkshire waggons; we had six of them and they were poled for two horses. Yorkshire waggons didn't have shafts like those in the south and in other parts of the country, they had a single pole which ran up between the horses. Three tons was a top load for two horses here; they were able to do a bit more than in many areas because the ground is mostly flat round here. With a very big and sound waggon – and it really did have to be sound, or it would pull apart – we might use three horses, putting the extra horse on the front pole using special iron hooks. It's maybe worth mentioning that in this area a cart always has two wheels and a waggon four. They were mostly made of local oak.

'For most of the winter we would be ploughing, because at that time of the year it was such a slow old business; but it gave a lot of men employment through the long winter months, and there wasn't much else to do in the cold months except perhaps keep an eye on the sheep, bring in the turnips for them, hedging and ditching – and a hundred and one other things! Roving bands of Irishmen would come each year to offer to do the hedging and ditching; they slept rough mostly, and Lord knows how they made a living, going from farm to farm doing it. It was very hard work, digging out the mud and slime and laying or cutting the hedge.

'A good team of men might lay a hundred feet of hedge in a day, and it was a really skilled business because the upright shoots in the hedge had to be carefully selected and then cut, but no more than three-quarters of the way through – any more and they would almost certainly die; you wanted them cut through just enough to make sure you could bend them down till they were parallel with the ground. Stakes were driven into the ground at intervals of a few feet, and then the pleachers – the three-quarters-severed uprights – would be brought down and woven through the stakes. The result looked rather bleak in winter, a bit like a sort of woven basket about three feet high, but when the branches started to shoot the following spring you had a marvellous stock-proof hedge that was always thick at the base. Modern hedges are often gappy and thin near the ground because the modern hedge-cutter just smashes the tops off.'

After winter ploughing and sowing in spring came harvest-time, which was really the high point of the farming year. Until the 1950s, massive ricks were built at Neswick Farm, and John still had a photograph showing the last rick, a testament, as he said, to a skill already by then in its death-throes.

'Some of the threshing was done straight after harvest, and the rest was spread through the winter. We used a steam thresher which was introduced in the nineteenth century: you just fed the sheaves of barley or whatever from the rick into it, and the men who did this work were known as stackers. Most of the winter threshing was done after the wheat was sown, in December. We'd do about forty days' threshing in all, perhaps one or two days a week, and it was generally all done by April, except perhaps for the last stack of oats which was kept for the horses.

'Until about 1950, everything was brought into the stackyard where it was stacked by the stackman: he laid the sheaves when they came in off the waggon, with a technique rather like brick-laying, as if he were building a wall. The middle wads were always kept slightly fuller than the outside ones, and what we called a spread fork was used for the work; it was slightly different in design from a pitchfork, less likely to hold the hay and better for spreading.

'The hayrick itself, well, it was a bit like a long, low house. It had to be perfectly symmetrical and the outside sheaves had to be at the correct angle if the whole thing was to be watertight, and if it wasn't watertight, it was worse than useless. Some stacks had perpendicular ends, others round ends. If we were building a big stack it would take all day, but the rick-builders were always kept busy because we used three waggons right through the day: while one was being loaded in the field, one was on the road to the stackyard, and one was being unloaded. One man stayed on the stack to build it, and one man, sometimes two, forked up the sheaves to the builder. At the eaves the stack might be ten feet tall.

'Come the spring, we would start drilling and cultivating, probably in early March if it was dry enough. Then it was all hands to the harrowing. We might finish by April, and there might be a little late ploughing into April for the turnips.

'After April, if you grew spuds you would plant them and then, in early June, we'd sow a few more turnips. As the crops started to come up we were busy chopping out the weeds. Weeds were bad, then, without chemicals and it was a full-time job just to keep on top of them.

'The farming year was very repetitive, but what we did was based on the experience of generations, and to vary it was hardly even thought about; though we might change the timing of one or two tasks by a month or so according to the state of the weather.'

While the arable year moved gradually on, the sheep and other animals still had to be looked after. The sheep were shorn at the end of May or the beginning of June, and although the Elgeys employed a shepherd on the farm full-time, there was so much extra work that they had to employ extra labour to help him at this time. And of course, as with everything else, the farmer's sons had to help, too.

'I did a lot of shearing when I was young, and I still demonstrate how it's done by hand today because with each passing year there are fewer and fewer of us who can do it; and many who can do it, can really only do it if they use electric shears. I used to use the old steel blades, which was strenuous work but not difficult once you knew how; I learned how to do it from the old shepherd, when I suppose I would have been about sixteen or seventeen.

'We had very heavy sheep here, pure Leicesters, but there are none now and we've gone in for something a little more trendy, Angora goats; but we still have to go for what's profitable because we still have to make enough money to pay the rent on the farm – we've never owned it; we're just tenants.

'Our regular shepherd gave up in the 1970s. There's little money in sheep now, and even when we had them in great numbers the regular farm men didn't like them. Don't ask me why, but they were always disliked. At one time we had as many as two hundred breeding ewes. Originally this was a mixed farm, as most were in the county, which had pigs, cattle and sheep, and grew wheat, oats, barley, beans and a few potatoes. Without chemical fertilisers we had to grow the crops in strict rotation to keep the land good; for example not more than two crops of wheat were ever grown in succession – if you tried a third year, the crop would be very poor, so after two years you'd sow what we called a break crop. It might go like this; you'd start with wheat, then barley, then you'd grow turnips, then the following winter you'd put sheep in on the turnips; then you'd sow oats, undersown with clover. The sheep would follow and then you'd be back to wheat. It was all carefully worked out to exploit the land while at the same time enriching it.'

But while they enriched the soil, at times the Elgeys found it increasingly difficult to avoid financial collapse.

'In the 1920s and 1930s we saved every penny we made, which wasn't much. Probably the worst time was in 1925, when my father had to go to the landlord and say we would leave because we just couldn't make the place pay: the cost in time and labour of producing corn and vegetables was far greater than the money we were able to raise by selling our things. The landlord, all credit to him, understood how difficult things were so he told my father that if he couldn't pay the rent, then he didn't have to. "Stay and do the best you can," he said, "and pay me the rent when you can." Our landlord was a Mr Rangham, and the Ranghams had been landlords here for generations. He was generous, although at the same time we knew he would never have been able to let the farm to anyone else.

'So my father had it at no rent for a few years and he was very careful with what little money he did make – other farmers round about spent freely and went bust.

'But if times were hard for us, they were very hard indeed for the farm-workers who had a terrible time; and though I think and hope we treated them as well as we could, they were often so poor that many couldn't even afford a bicycle – the cowman walked a mile from the village every day, and although he started at seven he was never late and he worked through till six. When the clocks changed he ignored them, because messing about with times had no effect on the cows and therefore none on his work. Robert Harper was his name.'

The number of farm-workers who died, worn out and broken by the lack of work and by endless grinding poverty in the 1920s, is difficult to calculate today. And with only the most rudimentary system of welfare, there is no doubt that tens of thousands of families in remote rural areas scraped by at a level of poverty quite unimaginable today. For days on end they might have only soup made with potato peelings; for fuel they would have to scour the woods and fields to collect sticks, and the head of the family might disappear for weeks on end tramping miles and sleeping in haystacks in search of a few days' work. Poverty can never have been easy to bear, but there is little doubt that people's expectations of a reasonable standard of living were lower in the early part of the twentieth century.

'Certainly people never worried about travel,' says John. 'The first bus came to nearby Bainton in about 1925, and before that everyone walked everywhere unless they had a cart or a waggon or could get a lift on one. But people very rarely went anywhere outside their immediate locality because there was nothing to go to, unless you had to travel for work or go on some specific business; in fact people thought it was an expensive or time-consuming nuisance if they had to go somewhere. The idea of travel for pleasure was beyond most people.

'But that first bus was a pretty sight. It had a beautifully made wooden and brass body which could be lifted right off the iron chassis, so when the man who ran it needed to cart pigs and sheep he manoeuvred the bus under a beam in his barn and used a block

and tackle to lift up the wooden coach body. Then he'd leave that hanging there and lower a different wooden body onto the chassis, in which he could cart animals.

'A carrier – a sort of travelling salesman – came to us once a week with all kinds of provisions. He'd call to collect our surplus butter and eggs, and then deliver them in Driffield for us at various destinations, shops and so on; he'd tell them where the produce had come from, and later on the shopkeepers would pay us. It was all done on trust. We'd pay the carrier a certain amount for doing the carrying, and that was how he made his living. He would take anything into town for anyone. Often you'd see him moving slowly along the lanes in his cart, and a typical load would be two women at the front, a dead sheep in the back and a great tub of our butter balanced in the middle.

'The carrier would take any sheep that had died on the farm, and it didn't matter if it had died from illness or accident or whatever. He'd take it to a small factory in Driffield where a man would skin it and take the wool off – there was a bit of money in that – and then the carcase would be put into a boiler for a few hours; the fat produced would be used for greasing wheels and axles on carts and waggons, or for making soap and face cream. I often thought of those girls carefully putting on face cream that had been made from a sheep we'd found dead in a ditch!

'Most villages and towns had men who set themselves up in this carcase-boiling business, and although it might sound a bit unpleasant it provided a living at a time when a living could be difficult to come by. People found ways to make a living in all sorts of ways that you just don't come across now: there were rat catchers and mole catchers, rabbit sellers, hedgers and ditchers. These have all gone now because people aren't prepared to live at such a low level, and things are better now in that sense. Of course, in some ways this means that nowadays we are very wasteful; in the example I've described, we used to get a little money for a dead sheep, and the man who took it off us got a little money for turning it into something useful. Now we have to pay someone to get rid of a carcase which is just disposed of uselessly.

'Today farming and most of life is completely tied up in rules and regulations, and in that respect things were very different when I was a young man. Farming wasn't nearly so scientific then, and a farmer relied on doing things the way they had always been done. That was all he knew, and innovations came in very slowly and were resisted; even motor transport and motor tractors were resisted by many farmers for years. For example a huge number of farmers still used horses in the 1950s when tractors were certainly available as early as the 1920s; but they felt safe with the old ways, and besides, they couldn't afford the capital outlay needed for a tractor. With a horse you just bred another one when you needed it.

'Horse transport was rarely, if ever, used to move other animals; that would have seemed a mad idea when the sheep, or cattle or whatever it might be, all had four good legs and could walk themselves wherever you wanted to get them. We used to take our sheep to Southburn station about six miles away; now the sheep are gone and so has the railway. In fact the countryside has changed from being a bustling, busy place to being underpopulated, with only a few people on the farms and in the villages and everyone travelling long distances to work.

'All the roads and lanes were well hedged in my early

days, and if your animals got into someone's garden as you drove them along the road it was the householder's fault if his roses were eaten. These days if your cattle eat someone's roses it's your fault. Cattle were walked regularly from Scotland to Smithfield Market in London, and townspeople were used to seeing animals about the town.

'I remember Dad buying cattle in York market, which was along the old wall of the city; the cattle would be milling around in the road and Dad would bargain with the owner. I remember once he bought some Irish store bullocks which had been driven all the way from Liverpool across to York on the roads. And after we bought them they were walked to the farm along the roads.

'Though farm work was hard in the 1930s no one ever worked on Sundays unless it was very urgent indeed. Now, because so few people work on the farms you have to work on Sundays pretty regularly. But the work isn't as hard physically now – in the 1930s you were following a plough or tossing hay all day with a fork so you had to have a day off just to recover, quite apart from any religious commitment.

'A lot of workers were itinerant: every year at harvest-time in August and September bands of men would come and were contracted for a month's work. Often they would have walked here from the Yorkshire Dales where the haymaking was a little earlier. Many men came to the same farms year after year, and their sons followed them; after leaving us they would go down to Lincolnshire for the potato-picking, and that way they gradually walked round the country picking up the seasonal jobs, as they picked them up year after year.

'These days a lot of our hedges are gone; you need them if you have sheep and so on, but for the big machines we use now they are a bit of a nuisance. We don't lose land here when the wind blows so we don't need hedges to prevent erosion as they do on some farms.'

The Elgeys had been farmers since the early 1700s. From his own research John had discovered that the family was first recorded at a 400-acre farm on the Yorkshire Wolds, about eight miles from Bainton, and he believed they would have taken that first farm soon after the great enclosures of the late eighteenth century. 'I know it was land that had never been farmed before,' he said. 'It was wasteland when they started, we know that. They owned that farm, but it was bought for what was called "three lives", in other words for three generations only; then it went back to the original owner. This was true of many farms in those days. We were in an odd situation here, too, because although we rented this farm, Dad owned another one nearby that someone else worked. He sold that farm during the Second World War, however, which was probably a mistake.

'My father died just after the war ended and I ran the farm until my nephew took over. Although I have no children of my own, I like to think it will be carried on by a member of the family when I'm gone.'

The Hiring Fair

I'll always mind the morning I first left home to go to the Lagan; that was what we called the country-side beyond the mountains where boys went on hire.

We made a lot of noise along the road, but there was still plenty of walk in us when we had finished the thirty-seven miles to Balleybofey. We lodged in a sort of barn, twenty-six boys of us on a shake down on the floor. The old-fashioned fellows who went over the roads before advised us to take off our shirts to save ourselves from vermin. In the hurry in the morning the shirts got mixed up, but the one I got was as good as the one I lost.

When we reached Strabane we all cuddled together and were scared at first but the big fellows told us to scatter out so as the farmers would see us. They made us walk up and down to see how we were set up and judge what mettle was in us. Anybody who looked tired or faulty in any way was passed over. The strong boys were picked up quickly and I was getting scared I would be left. In the end two men came to me.

'Well,' said one of them. 'Wee fellow, what wages do you want for the six months?'

I said, 'Three pounds ten.'

He said, 'Get out, you would be dear at your meat. Walk up there to the market clock until I see what you are like.'

I heard him whispering to the other fellow, 'He is wee, but the neck is good,' and he then offered me two pounds ten.

The other man caught both our hands in his, hit our hands a slap and said, 'Bought and sold for three pounds.'

Patrick Gallegher, *Paddy the Cope*, 1912

Button Hooks & Britches

AUBREY CHARMAN

HORSMAN, SUSSEX

*A*ubrey Charman farmed one of the oldest holdings in Sussex. Great House Farm has stared across the fields towards Southwater, a few miles south of Horsham in Sussex, since the middle decades of the fifteenth century. In 1462 according to the date carved on an oak beam, the oldest part, still largely unaltered, was put up by a local yeoman farmer. What is laughingly described as the new part of this massive timber-framed house was erected a little more than a century later, in 1575 (again the date appears on a beam) and this is still known as the 'new house'. What used to be an external door in one wall of the 1462 part of the house has been beautifully preserved since being enclosed in 1575 by the building of the new.

Aubrey Charman's family had farmed at Great House since 1823 when his great-great-grandfather came to Southwater. Though he knew little about this long-departed ancestor, other than that he was called James and that he was a good farmer, Aubrey still had the bill of sale from the farmer from whom the first of the Charmans took over the tenancy. Among the listed items were 'five cows in profit, three broad wheel dung carts, a cider press and four horses (three heavy)'. Since the date of that sale, September 1823, no farm sale had ever been held at Great House Farm; which is no doubt why in Aubrey's time it was still filled with the furniture and effects carried through the doors so long ago.

'No, we've never sold anything,' said Aubrey with a smile. 'But it's such an old place that I've come across all sorts of ancient objects since I've been here.' To illustrate his point he picked up a tiny, beautifully made child's leather shoe. 'It was probably made early in the nineteenth century,' he said. 'Perhaps about the time my great-great-grandfather arrived.' Other objects include an ancient longcase clock, tables and chests-of-drawers made by local craftsmen in the sixteenth and seventeenth centuries, button hooks, old harness, leather britches, and tools and iron implements of every conceivable shape and variety. But where on earth have they all come from?

'A lot of 'em from the roof,' said Aubrey with a grin. 'This house has fifteen bedrooms, and the roof space alone would fit two or three semi-detached houses! It's enormous, and though each stone slate weighs more than a hundredweight there are so many massive oak timbers the whole thing has hardly moved in four hundred years.'

The kitchen still had its flagged stone floor and massive lead pump. The pump was beautifully decorated with a floral motif raised in the lead, and was made when the house was built. Two oak settles were built into the walls of the massive fireplace, above which a remarkable ancient jack spit remained. Built with a weight on a pulley, the jack spit has a crude, clock-like series of wheels and gears, and with the weight attached will slowly turn the massive roasting spit above the fire. So ingenious is the design that the weight takes about fifteen minutes to reach the ground; during that time the housewife would have been able to get on with other tasks, safe in the knowledge that her roasting pig would be cooked evenly on all sides!

Aubrey spent most of his later years at work in the house but particularly in the massive sitting room. Situated immediately above the cellar, the room still had its original oak panelling.

'My father and I were both born in this house, and as I've said, we know little about great-great-grandfather other than that he was called James, that he came here in 1823 and he was a good farmer. In those days it was a mixed farm with hogs and sheep, corn and vegetables, and when I arrived in the world it was still pretty much the same with pigs and sheep and twenty cows, and we grew corn; we had about a hundred acres of corn. Now, however, we have ninety cows and no corn at all — you have to specialise now. My grandfather is buried in Southwater church and his seven children were all born here in this house. There were no midwives then, and there were still none when I was born.

'One or two village women would come up when Mother was about to have a child. The only doctor we had when I was young was in Horsham, four miles away, and that was too far. My grandfather's eldest son went away to Africa and became a butcher; my father was the second son, so he took over the farm. Dad was very clever; he was told he should have been a teacher.'

Aubrey is extremely proud of his father, and with reason. The old man was a talented mathematician, and studied a great deal at a time when few farmers would bother with such academic pursuits, as Aubrey explained: 'He studied farming far more than most. At a time when most farmers could get barely a couple of gallons of milk a day out of a cow, Dad was getting up to eight gallons which is as much as they can manage today. He had a book on protein, you see, and knew about its importance while everyone else went on unthinkingly as they'd always done. He fed those cows on Egyptian cotton seed cake which is about 42 per cent protein, very high. And linseed cake, which he thought was good too, and so it was. I still have his protein book, and it even tells you how much protein there is in an oak leaf!'

Aubrey's earliest memories were of the hard winters of long ago, and of leading two massive horses up an icy field. His father kept a team of Shires: 'Seven cart horses, I recall. I'd have been about ten when I first remember leading them. Always slowly, always at a walk. A carthorse never runs or trots, but they'll do three miles an hour and the smallest boy can lead and stop them when they're trained. Ours were trained by the farm-workers; normally we had eight farm-workers, and two pupils who would generally have been eighteen or perhaps nineteen. We had farm cottages then, too, which have gone now, but each man had a cottage with the job in the early days, and we never turned them out when they retired; they stayed till they died, or went into a home.

'Winters were undoubtedly worse when I was young, and summers better than now – Father had always finished the harvest by the time we were just starting in my day. We still have the dates the harvest finished carved on our granary wall, and they go back more than a hundred years.

'In winter we always skated on the pond in front of the house for weeks on end; now, the ice is never thick enough. We used to skate late into the evening when the moon – or as we called it, the parish lantern – was out.

There is an exception to that, however: 1963. That was a terrible winter.'

As Aubrey remembered, all traffic came to a halt around Southwater in 1963, so deep were the roads and lanes in snow. The farm milk couldn't be collected, and after three days all the farm churns were full, because, of course, the cows had still to be milked. But Aubrey had the answer: 'With sixteen full churns my wife and I toured every street in Southwater in the cart. I rang a big bell and shouted "Milk!" at the top of my voice, and people came out and stopped us, and my wife filled their cans and jugs as required. As they hadn't had a delivery for three days they were more than happy. We sold 160 gallons that morning, and it was as if the clock had gone back fifty years to a time when we would have sold all our milk locally.'

The Charmans have always rented Great House Farm. They tried to buy it on two or three different occasions, but each time, according to Aubrey, the landlord's agent boosted the price to an exorbitant level. 'Sixty years ago it was valued at £25,000, but the agent, who was always on the grab, said we couldn't have it for less than £56,000. It's funny, too, because although we've been here a long time the landlord's family has been here even longer. Sir John Aubrey Fletcher owns it now, and it's been in his family since 1678.'

Aubrey was fascinated by the past, but this didn't mean he rejected everything the modern world had to offer.

'Horse ploughing was a skilled business, but so is ploughing with a tractor. An untrained man couldn't do it. You have to know what you're doing when you set the plough, although I would admit that with a modern plough once you've set it correctly it's pretty easy.

'The difficulties of the past may sound interesting today, but when modern alternatives came along I can see why people often grabbed them gratefully with both hands. Take matches – well, they weren't invented till the 1850s; before that you had to strike a flint to light anything, and getting a flame from a flint wasn't easy. We got round the problem here by never letting the fire go out – year after year it stayed alight, and there was a skill, too, in making sure it stayed alight. Every night when you went to bed you covered the glowing ashes with grey, burned-through ash; in the morning when you raked this grey stuff off, the red embers would still be alight and you could get the fire going again.

'We had two maids in those days who slept at the top of the house. They got up at six every morning – the same time as everyone else – and lit the big sixty-gallon copper we had for boiling water; and this copper had to be filled using buckets filled at the pump. That carried on until about 1940 when piped water arrived, but the well and the pump are still just as good as they ever were. So is the pond, and let me tell you, it isn't just any old pond: it was built about a hundred years ago chiefly for washing the farm horses' legs, which is why it's got a solid stone bottom. When they're ploughing, heavy horses get their legs badly caked with mud, in particular the long hair above the hoofs, and if it isn't cleaned off they get a terrible skin affliction we called farcy. So every evening at ploughing time they'd be tied nose to tail and led to the pond, and then they'd be driven round it for a few minutes until all the mud on their legs had washed off. The youngest ploughman normally rode the first horse round and round to make it go and the others would follow. We did this right through ploughing time until we got out first tractors, though I never heard of any other farmers doing it.

'Horses were used for some odd tasks in my youth, things that people have forgotten all about. For example, until 1914 two huge Shire horses were always kept at Horsham station to shunt trucks into sidings. These trucks might easily weigh twenty tons, but the horses were specially trained to lean against the trucks until they started to move. Very few horses could do it.'

In the early years of the twentieth century the roads, train stations and canal sides were places where you would see horses busy at work, but the farmhouse itself was also a place of intense daily activity, as Aubrey recalled: 'My family consisted of my parents and us five children – I was second to youngest – but the house had other occupants, too. Among the staff would be a housemaid and dairymaid, who would help milk the cows and clean the dairy utensils. Every day two large pails of milk were put through the separator to separate the cream from the skim milk; the latter was fed to the calves until they were eight weeks old – all the female calves were kept to go into the dairy herd when they were mature at about three years old.

'The house had a set weekly routine: on Mondays the housemaid would light the big sixty-gallon copper fire with faggots, bundles of hazel sticks about six feet long and a foot wide, to heat the water for washing day. At about 9am every Monday two of the workers' wives would help to do the weekly wash, and that happened every Monday right through my childhood and beyond.

'There was also a huge baking oven in our kitchen, and here bread was baked every Tuesday: always Tuesday.

Three faggots were pushed into the seven-foot-long brick oven, then set alight; when the embers were glowing red hot, about twenty big lumps of dough were placed above the embers, using a long- handled shovel called a baker's peel. Then the cast-iron door was closed to keep in the heat. Twenty minutes later, the dough would be baked into lovely crusty cottage loaves – the smell was wonderful, and we boys were often given a still-hot slice to eat. You didn't need butter or jam when the bread was fresh from the oven like that, made from home-grown wheat milled between huge millstones at the Southwater windmill, and later at Warnham water-driven corn mill. Some yeast would be saved to mature for the next week's bake. My mother looked after all the baking, and several of the labourers were given loaves as part of their wages.

'Wednesday was always butter-making day. My mother had been trained in this art before she was married, so she was an expert, churning the cream into butter in what we called an end-over-end churn. It usually took about two hours, and a man was always on hand to help turn the handle because it was hard work after a while. And by the time the dairy equipment had been scrubbed and packed away, another day had gone; but that's why different days were allocated to the different major tasks around the house and farm. Thus Thursday was ironing day, and Friday general shopping day.

'On Friday my father would harness the pony and bring round the trotting cart to deliver some of the butter and eggs to shops in Horsham. As we went round we'd buy the things that we needed, although when I was young you couldn't buy vegetables in any shops because everyone grew their own, so there was no market for them.

'Saturdays were busy because we had to get double supplies of hay and straw ready for the cattle for Sunday. No work other than feeding – both stock and humans – was done on a Sunday, and most people went to church, sometimes twice; all the children went to Sunday school on Sunday afternoons, and there was always an annual outing to the seaside for them. I would say that until the first war most farmers and country people went to church on Sunday, and if they weren't there the vicar would want to know why. But generally people were pleased to go because most couldn't read and it was the only way they got to hear any stories; it was also the way village people kept in touch with each other. Remember, too, that if you lived in the country before the Great War there was nothing else at all to do except work. So church was really a bit of a break from the routine.

'Twice a year my Father would kill a big pig for our own consumption. Outside our kitchen door there was a large square of flat bricks with a drain, laid out specially for killing pigs; it is still there now. A pig would be selected and a cord tied on one of its hind legs so if it tried to run away or misbehave it was easier to control, and it would then be driven from the sty to the back door. Here it was blindfolded, stunned with a very heavy hammer, rolled on its back and its main jugular vein cut. After being bled, it was scrubbed and all its bristles removed. It was hung up and cut into joints, some being hung up the chimney to be smoke-dried by that great log fire which was never allowed to go out. The belly parts were salted down in a huge chest that we called the brine tub, and about sixty pounds of salt would be used for the belly pork from one pig; the salt stopped it going bad. Bellypork was a luxury for the farm-workers when they came in to tea at haymaking time. To be honest, I think the way we killed our pigs was very humane even by modern standards; because they were blindfolded they never really knew what was happening.

'There's a funny story connected with pork to tell you. My wife and I were sitting in the dining-room one day in 1966 when a great big piece of soot crashed down the chimney and onto the dining-room floor. My wife picked it up and threw it out of the window into the garden; but then later that same day we saw the dog was taking a particular interest in it, so we went to investigate. And would you believe it, that piece of soot turned out to be a great big piece of bacon that had been hung up the chimney to smoke at least twenty years earlier by my father. We cleaned the sooty meat and tasted it, and it was delicious!

'Eight farm-hands sat at the table for tea at five o'clock when haymaking was in full swing in the old days. They had homemade bread and cold belly pork, homemade cheese and butter, washed down with homemade cider. Only half an hour was allowed for this meal, as all hay was pitched by hand in those days. We have a big cellar and can still smoke our own bacon up the chimney. I remember long strings of sausages hanging on hooks close to the ceiling along the beams; they would hang there until they were all used, and they never seemed to go bad.

'We had forty apple trees and a cider press, so when the corn was stacked in the stackyard after harvest, the men were sent to gather the apples. The best eating apples were laid out on newspaper, carefully and individually in the attic. The sour apples were crushed in the cider press and all the juice collected, treated with yeast and other ingredients, and put into forty-gallon barrels. We usually made over one hundred gallons of cider each year, as this was the drink sent out to the men working in the hot sun during the hay and corn harvests. The cider barrels were stacked in our cellar and I still have some thirty gallons maturing now, seventy years after they were first put down there. These days the farm-workers prefer tea, which is surprising because they always seemed to enjoy the cider so much.'

Aubrey had records of his family's movements going back to 1749, but these only begin to include substantial details in the middle decades of the twentieth century. His great-grandfather, for example, was the first warden of the village church, which was built in 1850. His father sang in the same church choir for seventy years, and Aubrey himself sang there regularly every Sunday throughout his life. He stepped down from full-time farming in his eighties when his son took over.

Throughout his stories of the past Aubrey acknowledged that life in rural Sussex before and just after the Great War had changed little from what it would have been centuries earlier. He was particularly conscious of this because the lives of his own ancestors were so well documented. In the same way that Great House Farm passed from father to son down the generations, so too were many other local businesses and trades handed on from one generation to the next. The trades of wheelwright and farrier, for example, were often carried on by men whose great-great-grandfathers had started their own businesses. As Aubrey recalled:

'Before the first war there were two blacksmith's shops in Southwater, one run by Mr Gardner and one by Mr Piper. Piper also made waggons and waggon wheels, and many times I have watched him and his men make a cartwheel rim out of iron. This would be heated in the forge until it was red hot, then forced onto a newly made wheel; the heat would make the metal expand, but even then it would be a tight fit and would have to be hammered on. As soon as the rim was fitted, five or six buckets of cold water would be thrown over it to make it shrink; so you can imagine how tightly it finally gripped the wheel! These wheels were so tight and well-made they might run for fifty years with perhaps only two changes of rim in all that time.

'I also remember John Piper buying one particular group of oak trees; when he cut them down he sent one to be cut into paper-thin veneer because he knew that this particular tree had a lovely flower, or pattern, on it. This was in about 1933, and do you know, that oak tree went to veneer about forty rooms and cabins on the Queen Mary.

'Piper also made coffins for the village people, and would

arrange the whole funeral including organising a farmer to transport the coffin in a waggon to the church. In fact the last villager who died and was taken to church in a waggon was my mother. She died in 1944, and I remember my father washed his newest four-wheeled Sussex waggon and took her in it from the farmhouse to the church. Even by then this was unusual because motor hearses were already in common use.

'When I was six I remember coming out of Southwater Infants School and seeing the Horsham fire engine for the first time: drawn by horses, it thundered past the school and we raced after it all the way down the road to Cripplegate where the village windmill was on fire; but as the windmill was all wood it had virtually vanished up in smoke by the time the engine arrived.'

The Cripplegate windmill was one of the last of England's movable wind-driven mills. These movable mills were built on oak skids as much as thirty feet long, and as many as sixteen oxen were harnessed to them when the mill was sold to another village or if it had to be moved for any reason.

'Oxen were used,' remembers Aubrey 'because they were slow and steady, and would never rush, and that meant there was little danger of the mill being pulled over when it was being dragged across hilly terrain.' The Cripplegate windmill that Aubrey watched being destroyed by fire all those years ago was so called because it started life at Cripplegate, one of medieval London's gateways. Centuries old already, in 1810 it was towed slowly by oxen from London to Rusper village about six miles north of Horsham. In 1823 it was moved to Southwater, again using oxen. But if oxen were slow, the same thing couldn't always be said of horses. 'Contrary to modern belief, horses could be very fast indeed. You'd be surprised at the distances a good horse used to cover in a day – not cart-or farm-horses, but a good trotting pony. I'll give you an example: my uncle had a fine horse, and three or four times a year he'd harness this horse to the dogcart and trot up to us from his house about twenty-five miles away. The horse could do twelve miles an hour, so it only took him about two hours to get to us. He'd spend the day and then drive back in two hours, and in spite of a round trip of fifty miles and a good smart pace all the way, the horse would never get in a lather.'

Farmers are marvellously innovative when it comes to avoiding waste, and Aubrey's ancestors were no exception. Thus when a giant cask of homemade cider was spoiled when air leaked into it, Aubrey's father fed the forty-five gallons, little by little, to his pigs. Each time the pigs emptied the trough they very quickly became completely stupefied, and fell asleep until their next feed. 'This went on for six weeks, and for the whole time those pigs were completely drunk,' said Aubrey with a grin. 'But the pigs grew so quickly on this diet that my father contacted a Horsham brewer and bought spoiled beer from him regularly!

'Animals are strange things, though. One of the oddest occasions I can remember was when a big sow we had became ill with pneumonia and apparently died. We dragged it onto the stable-manure heap, and being so heavy it was quickly half submerged by manure; Father and I planned to take it to the carcase man the following day because we would at least get a few shillings for it. But when we went to look for that pig next day we found it was alive and well and back in the pig house! All we could think was that the heat from the manure had driven the pneumonia out of it and revived it!'

Many of the everyday items of food that we now take for granted were difficult, if not impossible, to obtain early in the twentieth century. Other items such as fish were a rare treat for inland families like the Charmans. 'Over the years from 1920 until about 1936 we children would listen out for the sound of a bell ringing on the main Worthing Road. Immediately we heard it, my mother would give me a shilling and tell me to run up to the road because it was the mackerel seller, a man with a big horse-drawn cart piled high with thousands of mostly mackerel and herrings. He would have started early that morning on the south coast, and gradually worked his way towards London selling his fish at every village along the way. We usually got thirty herrings for a shilling, and sometimes more if there were only a few left, because by the time he reached us, the fish man would usually have had enough and would not be wanting to go further. If he did, he had to go up Picks Hill at Horsham which was very steep; in fact it was much steeper than it is today, and to get up it you had to hire two extra horses at the foot of the hill at the toll gate; they were kept there specifically for this purpose. You can still see how steep the hill originally was if you look at the two sides of the cutting the council made to reduce its steepness.

'Between 1915 and about 1935 there was another oddity on the road, one which almost everyone forgets these days: the steam engine. The steamers, as they were known, needed a lot of water so village ponds near the road were kept as free as possible of rubbish so they could fill up as they went along.'

Aubrey would have been the first to agree that in the old days the countryside produced many eccentrics. They were usually tolerated, however quirky their behaviour might become, but it is wrong to think that they were always amusing and some were simply reclusive. Aubrey remembers one noted Southwater character whose reputation as an eccentric was based largely on the fact that he was extremely antisocial:

'Bernard Green died in 1979. He would have been about seventy-five, I think, but I remembered him from when he was twenty and he came to work for my father. He was a most conscientious worker, but nothing would induce him to get to work before nine o'clock and as that upset all the other farmworkers who started at seven, we had to get rid of him. When he left he rented about twenty acres of land and reared stock. But he would help any farmer at harvest-time. He was often seen digging potatoes late at night by the light of a lamp, but you'd never see him doing it during daylight. He never mixed with the villagers, and lived in some poverty in a cottage in New Road. He was often seen returning from his cattle well after midnight. When finally he was found dead he was in his bed with his overcoat and boots on, and all around him were scattered cattle sales cheques going back years which he'd never bothered to pay into the bank. Although he lived in Southwater for more than sixty years I don't suppose he was known to more then twenty people, and he had no friends.

'Animals can be eccentric, too; each one has its own character, and occasionally you'll get one that is remarkable in some way – like our mare Dolly. She was used as a trace horse: when we were carting mangolds or whatever from a very wet field, the waggon would sink into the mud; so using a special chain harness we would add Dolly to the horse already harnessed to the waggon. When the load had been pulled across the field to the hard road, the man in charge would unhitch Dolly, hang the chains over her back and turn her round. She'd then set off on her own across the field precisely to the front of the next loaded cart, and she would do this all by herself twenty times a day. She was a lovely horse with a marvellous nature, and she worked for us for twenty-three years before we pensioned her off.

'Another horse we had wasn't so amenable. She used to be in a terrible hurry to get out of her harness and start feeding when we tried to unhitch her in the evenings; she got so bad that she'd sometimes break out of the harness, and we knew that eventually someone would get hurt. We cured her by putting a coat over her head before unhitching her and leading her to within a couple of feet of the stable wall. Of course she bolted as usual, but this time she hit the wall and knocked herself out – but she never rushed again.

'Horses could be marvellous. Every morning our seven would be tied together, and entirely on their own they would leave the stable in line and walk eighty yards down to the pond to drink before returning to the stable for breakfast. They always did the whole thing on their own, at the same pace and in the same time. It was a marvel to see.

'Horsham market was started in 1852; it has long gone, but we used to go by horse, or on foot driving the sale animals, and it was a fair sight to see. There would be sheep, cattle, chickens and rabbits everywhere, and you would always see a number of Jews, who came down from London to buy poultry and rabbits.

'For as long as anyone could remember, and certainly until the end of the Second World War when new hygiene regulations made it impossible, most villagers kept a pig or two in a sty built at the bottom of the garden. They bought the smaller piglets, known as dolly pigs or runts, from a farmer's litter, and reared them on boiled scraps, milk, curds, and buttermilk. In the autumn they would go "gleaning" which was a family affair, to collect corn-heads spilled at harvesting. I've known a family collect several bushels of corn-heads which were fed to the pigs for several weeks. When half-grown, the pigs were sent to the butcher for killing. The butcher would buy half while the other half was taken back by the cottager to be smoked in the chimney for use during the winter. The same could be done today, except that modern law does not permit the smell of a pig in the garden in housing estates. The great thing about keeping a pig was that it didn't need much space and you could feed it on anything; we feed ours on dead chickens and dead rabbits with the feathers and fur on, bad cabbage and apples, damp corn going mouldy and absolutely any waste vegetables from the kitchen. They thrived on everything. I even remember one farmer whose land was infested with rabbits: every evening he took the Land Rover and his gun, and shot up to thirty rabbits which he then fed to his pigs, as meal at that time was very dear. For two months those pigs lived on unskinned, uncooked rabbits and what is more, looked very well on it. Pigs will eat almost anything, even bones, and can successfully convert any waste foods.

'Nowadays most farmers specialise in one or two products in a big way, where seventy years ago they would have kept a few of all types of livestock, including geese, turkeys and farmyard fowls. My grandfather and his father kept large black lop-eared pigs which were known as Sussex pigs. They were easy to control because their ears covered their eyes, which meant that if they tried to run off they would bang into things because they couldn't see! Our breeding sows were driven out every day to graze grass, and in the autumn walked to the woods to feed on acorns. As boys, my father and his brother used to take the pigs out to certain fields before they went to school each day, and they would fetch them back in the evening, after school.

'On one occasion, three of our sows were due to farrow at the same time, so one shed was filled with straw. The sows were brought in that night and they made a cosy hole in the straw. The next day they had all farrowed, so they were trough fed, near their young. Three days later the little pigs had all appeared and were running about, and there was a record number: fifty-one, seventeen per sow. The sows were sisters and happily suckled each other's piglets, so no one really knew the correct mothers or how many each mother had had. My father assured me these facts were true, so pigs have not improved in performance today since the average for the best herds is now ten and a half piglets reared. Black pigs have all but disappeared because modern housewives don't like the black pigment caused by the skin; also the Middle White, snub-nosed pigs which were very popular thirty years ago as they were good doers and very fat are now almost extinct, as people have gone off fat.'

Aubrey's memories of animal husbandry, and of the everyday life of farm and village in Edwardian times are remarkably precise. He even remembered seeing men wearing that most English of farmworkers' garments, the smock: 'For more than two hundred years all agricultural workers in Sussex and many other areas wore a smock – it was actually a kind of overcoat. It went out of use just after the Great War in this area, but I can remember the men wearing them. The Sussex smock was a long bell-shaped garment which had no buttons but had to be slipped over your head. They were rather heavy, especially when dressed with tallow – the fat from which candles were made – to make them waterproof. Nevertheless, if you were ploughing all day in the rain this waterproofing was a great asset. Most workers and farmers kept a second, clean white smock for attending church.'

Like many farmers and farm-workers who grew up during the early 1900s, Aubrey built up an immunity to TB, the disease that was once endemic in British cattle; in fact, either you became immune or you died.

'Our cows were first tested in the spring of 1920, and twenty-seven out of thirty were found to have TB; under the law, these had to be slaughtered. To my father and I this was a great disappointment as they looked perfectly healthy. It wasn't a total disaster, however, because we were given money in compensation for our loss. With this in his pocket, my father went to the north of England and bought replacement cows which had passed all the TB tests.

'Twelve months later, after the cows had been housed

all winter, a second test was carried out for TB, and imagine our disappointment when twenty-five out of thirty cows failed! My father promptly called in the vet, who phoned the head of the ministry's veterinary department; we received a visit from the ministry, and were told that we had to build an outside yard so that the air could blow through night and day. We could use the old enclosed cowshed for milking only: but should turn the cows out again into the outside yard as soon as fresh straw had been spread.

'What had been happening was this: a cow with what might have been dormant TB germs breathed against the wall of the cowshed, and in the hot, enclosed atmosphere the next cow caught the germs. She then passed it on to the next cow, and so on until virtually every cow was infected. Remember, the cows spent five months in this cow house, and evidently the temperature was so hot the TB spread very rapidly. On this clay soil all our cows must be housed for the five long winter months even today, but they are kept in open yards and we haven't had a case of TB in any animal for thirty years.

'To encourage farmers, in 1920 the Government paid an extra 4d per gallon for milk proved free of TB. But as a child I had a glass of milk for supper every night, and I must have drunk many a gallon of tubercular milk. Because nature builds an immunity to most diseases in children, I have remained very healthy, although I must admit I've never been tested for TB. I think cattle are now more healthy than most humans because they get tested for things so often.'

Among the most interesting medieval survivals that Aubrey remembered were the faggots used to light ovens and heat coppers. Faggots were bundles of wood about six feet long, tied in the centre, and about nine inches in diameter. For centuries in Sussex and elsewhere all bread was baked in ovens that had first been heated with faggots. Two or three bundles were set alight in the oven, which was usually brick-built and fitted in the side of the chimney. The faggots were allowed to burn down until they were just red-hot ashes, then the bread dough was placed on a tray on a long-handled shovel and put into the oven. Up to forty loaves could be cooked at once. One or two bakeries in Southwater were still using faggots up until about 1930; then gas came in and other heating methods were used.

'In Southwater in 1930 there was a thirty-four-acre piece of hazel woodland which stretched from Church Lane up to Shipley Comer. This was coppiced regularly every five years, in four-acre blocks, to supply faggots for our local baker, and for one or two other bakers in Horsham. Now the whole site has been built on, the Southwater baker carries on his trade in the same building, but using a modern oven.'

For Aubrey, one of the greatest losses to the late twentieth-century countryman was the rabbit: before the arrival of myxomatosis in the 1950s – 'it was introduced deliberately,' said Aubrey – most land workers had a ferret or two for catching rabbits, which represented a good and, most importantly, a free meal. A ferret would be put down the rabbits' bury after nets had been placed over every escape hole that could be discovered. 'The rabbits nearly always fled at the first whiff of the ferret, and as they shot out of their bury holes they were caught in the nets – though it was only occasionally as easy as that makes it sound! We caught a lot, but we also lost a lot. In Horsham's weekly market I used to see about three hundred rabbits for sale regularly. And rabbit skins were bought by the rag-and-bone men who came round every week; I was told the rabbit hair was used to make trilby hats.'

The attitude of country people to animals was clearly less sentimental in former times, but most country children always kept pets of various sorts, and then, as now, most farmers were unlikely to be without a dog. Aubrey remembered one or two rather more unusual animal companions: 'We had some marvellous pets over the years. My wife once reared an orphan lamb which became completely domesticated. People say it can't be done, but it can. The lamb came when it was called, would climb the stairs and jump on the bed, and it slept with the dogs. When we used to walk across the fields to the pub it came with us – we used to give it beer in a dish which it loved, and chocolate. Eventually it grew so big and greedy it became a terrible nuisance, and ate all the flowers in the garden. When it was three we had to sell it, and by then it weighed more than 150 pounds!

'At the moment, as well as my golden retriever I've got two cats. They sleep with the dog, and when the dog and I go to check the cows the cats come along with us – it must be two miles across the fields and back, but every week they make the journey. Animals are funny things. When I was in my thirties I had a dog that always ran up and down the furrow all day long when I was ploughing. Hour after hour it would run, never stopping and hardly ever even slowing down. I reckoned he must have run a hundred miles each day!'

There's no doubt that roads, housing estates and

modern farming practices had dramatically reduced the amount of wildlife in Aubrey's part of Sussex in his final years.

'Animals and birds that were once common exist now only in small pockets, and one or two species have disappeared altogether. In the 1920s I remember seeing quail and corn-crakes running in my father's corn, but there's hardly a corn-crake left in Britain now. I even caught one once! It had got caught in the binder and tied up in a sheaf of corn, so I fished it out and put it in my pocket. Soon it began to struggle, so I took it out and showed it to a friend who was nearby. Just as he took a look the bird's head flopped down and my friend insisted it was dead. I wasn't so sure, so I put it on the ground. Soon one eye opened, then the other and next minute it ran off! That was my only experience of an animal feigning death to escape trouble.'

Before the widespread use of chemical fertilisers, most of which arrived in rural Sussex in the years following the end of the Second World War, farmers had to rely on muck-spreading and marl. 'Everyone knows how good muck is on the land, but few people realise about marl. It's a sort of blue clay which you find perhaps fifteen or twenty feet down, and when it's spread thinly on pasture land it sweetens the grass beautifully – by that I mean it makes it far more palatable for the animals. We had our own marl pit, and every winter the carts would go back and forth to it all day long. Cartloads were spread over the more distant fields where no manure was available. The first half-decent alternative to marl arrived here in about 1910, in the form of sulphate of ammonia from the gasworks!'

In a world without television and radio, language and patterns of speech were little diluted by outside influences. For most of the inhabitants of Southwater, as late as the 1930s London was still a remote place, and many villagers would have spent their entire lives within the few square miles bounded perhaps by Horsham four miles to the north. This insularity produced a distinct Sussex dialect which has all but vanished.

'It's the fact that people are able to travel about more, and they hear different accents on television. That's what's got rid of it, but I can remember from my very early days bits and pieces of the local way of speaking. I'll give you an example: when I was about ten I asked the carter if I could lead one of the horses up the field, and I can still remember exactly what he said: "Keep they wheels in the lowses, don't knock no gaat posties and don't scat yer legs on they lawyers and don't get in the dick." It was a rich, wonderful sound you don't hear today – oh, and lowses are ruts, lawyers are brambles and a dick is a ditch.'

Aubrey was ambivalent about the changes he has seen in his lifetime. While he agreed that much that was good had vanished, he had a pragmatic attitude and accepted that things have to change. 'My great-grandfather would have made changes from the way his father farmed, as I've accepted my son has made changes from the way I did things. Life is like that and so is farming. You can't get the past back.'

One of Aubrey's strongest memories from his youth had only an indirect connection with farming, but it was a story he loved to tell: 'When I was seventeen I saw a Rolls Royce advertised for £30. My total savings amounted to £17 at the time, but I wrote to the advertiser anyway and offered him what I had, and to my astonishment he took it! My older brother drove it down from Leatherhead. It was a Silver Ghost built in 1912, and because it had a 45 horsepower engine I couldn't afford to tax it for the road; road tax in those days was worked out at £1 per year for every unit of horsepower. So all I could do was drive it round the meadows. A few years later I stripped the body off, wrapped chains round the rear axle and used it to roll and harrow the meadows. Then I got fed up with it and we left it in a shed for years. Eventually I sold the engine to a man who needed an engine for his motorboat, and I used the chassis as a chicken house. It's not every farmer who keeps his chickens in a Rolls!'

Custom in Sussex

The custom in Sussex is this: when a tenant quits a
farm he receives payment according to valuation, for
what are called dressings, the half-dressings, for seeds
and lays, and for the growth of underwood in coppices
and hedgerows; for the dung in the yards; and in short
for whatever he leaves behind him, which, if he had
stayed, would have been of value to him.

The dressings and half-dressings include, not only
the manure that has recently been put into the land, but
also the summer ploughings; and, in short, everything
that has been done to the land, and the benefit of which
has not been taken out again by the farmer. This is a
good custom because it ensures good tillage to the land.
It ensures also a fair start to the new tenant.

William Cobbett, *Rural Rides,* 1830

Two-way Traffic

Straw was a basic necessity for livestock farming,
providing litter for animals kept in stalls, sties or cattle
courts; oats, hay and straw were also sold for the stables
in the towns from which dung was returned by cart
and railway to the market towns in Hertfordshire,
Bedfordshire, Kent, Sussex and Worcestershire.

But this double trade, fodder and straw moving
from the farms into the towns and dung moving back,
is threatened as the motor car and the motor lorry
supplant the urban horse.

Agrarian History of England, 1934

SHEPHERD
& HORSEMAN

GEORGE GREENHELD

BILBOROUGH, NORTH YORKSHIRE

*G*eorge Greenheld spent most of his working life among the sheep and horses of the Yorkshire Wolds. He officially retired in the 1980s but for years the farmers in his part of Yorkshire knew that if they were having problems at lambing time, George was far more likely to be able to help than the local vet. For George was one of the old school, a man whose knowledge was based not on books and theory, but on a lifetime spent among the animals he tended. Born in Edstone near Kirby Moorside in 1923, his younger days were hard by any standards, but he always insisted that on the whole he had enjoyed a rich, fulfilling life.

'I don't think another generation will ever live through such changes again. When I was a lad you never saw a car, or if you did if was a real event. Everything was moved about on waggons, and a young lad knew he would do more or less as his father and grandfather had done as soon as he was old enough.' For generations the Greenhelds earned their living on the land or in occupations intimately connected with farm work and agriculture. George's grandfather, for example, was a waggon driver for a big grain mill at Pickering; he could neither read nor write, but worked diligently for many years carting grain from Pickering to Scarborough along the slow roads – and they were slow, as George explained:

'Shires and work horses had their own steady rhythm, and the pace of life was dictated by them. No one in those days moved faster than a horse could move.'

George's father farmed at Kirby Moorside and although many of George's memories of childhood were happy ones, his early years were marked by a series of disasters: 'My father was killed by a farm horse when I was just twelve years old. Mother left the farm after that and we went to live in a cottage in Pickering. But we were there only about a year when Mother died, too, and I was put out to work for some relatives. I don't want to go into that too much because they made my life hell – working there was one of the worst experiences of my life. They paid me £25 a year and tried to work me to death; it got so bad that eventually I ran away. They treated me like a slave. I was up at 5.30 every morning seven days a week, and had to work right through till six at night whatever the weather.'

What must have made the back-breaking, thankless tasks of those years much worse was the fact that George had been struck down by polio at about the time his father was killed. His brother fell victim to the disease at the same time and died, but George survived – just. He was helped by an uncle.

'The doctor in the hospital to which I was sent said that I would never be able to walk again – but then I didn't like that doctor much; I think he liked having us there so he could observe and experiment on us, and I don't think he thought of us as human beings. Anyway, he gave me no encouragement at all as I lay there unable to walk. An old uncle of mine helped me in the end – he worked as a gamekeeper and lived in an old cottage well off the road, and he agreed to have me when I came out of hospital. I couldn't walk then, so he met me where the bus put me down and carried me more than a mile on his back to his cottage. In the days that followed he made me two little walking sticks and told me I could certainly walk again if I just kept at it. And do you know, soon after that I was able to drop one stick and then the other. It was hard though, very hard. But once I was rid of the second stick I never looked back, and the fact that I have always walked with a bit of a limp has made not the slightest difference to my life. I've always done what I've wanted to do.'

Being his own man and able to do just as he pleased was clearly always important to George – 'I could always ride a horse as well as any man' he said proudly, which is why he eventually chose to flee from the farm where he had started work. 'They would have worked me to death otherwise, I think. I had to milk twelve cows and get the churns filled at the side of the road every day by eight o'clock, then clean out the byres and feed the cattle; then I had to go round the sheep, pull turnips and can fodder. The food was very poor, too. I put up with it for two years, and then a friend who worked on a big farm owned by the Hon George Vestey told me they needed a cattleman. So I rode over to them – eight miles on my bike – and the boss agreed to see me; as it was Martinmas week I was able to take the job they offered straightaway. The farmworker's term of employment ran from one Martinmas to the next in those days. My old boss told me he wouldn't let me go, so I packed my tin – all farm lads and labourers had tin trunks for their things in those days – and upped and left. I just ran for it.'

The new farm was a big improvement, and George was paid the splendid sum of thirty shillings a fortnight, plus overtime. After two bitter years as a slave to people who were supposed to be his family, it was a real relief. 'Oh, I was in clover there,' he said, with a beaming happy smile. 'Six men lived in and we all got along. They were older than me, but good honest men and so helpful. I had a bit more free time, too, so sometimes we used to go to the pictures at Pocklington on our bikes and then have fish and chips and a bottle of Vimto afterwards – and all for 1s 6d! We also played dominoes and cards in the evenings, but generally went to bed early; you had to, because you had to be up early again next day. We would visit the lads on other farms round about, too, and compare our masters and our situations. I spent three years at this farm. However, it was only when I left and moved to a farm near Scarborough that I came to work among horses. They'd been around before, of course, but then I was a cattleman and hadn't worked much with them.'

In fact George worked full time with horses at his next farm, Scalby Lodge; he had taken work there in order to be closer to his sister who had moved to Scarborough. The horses were his direct responsibility: 'I loved working with the horses. We'd get up at 5.30, groom them, feed them, and then go in for our own breakfast at 6.45. At 7.30 we'd get them harnessed and set off for the fields. Ploughmen often rode to the fields, though never sitting astride, always sideways on the horse. That slow morning ride was worth a lot to me, the gentle movement of the massive horse and the view from that height over the hedges and across the fields. We ploughed with a single-furrow plough, and with the horses side by side, one in the furrow and one on the land – that is, on the bit yet to be ploughed.'

George insisted that ploughing was a serious, skilled business, far more so than it would be with a modern tractor, because apart from the difficulties of controlling the horses, the old ridge-and-furrow technique involved cutting much deeper into the land than the more modern method. But although the work was hard, it had its compensations: 'Although you walked many miles in a day's ploughing it was lovely work, even if the weather was bad. You were out in the air, the gulls wheeling overhead, the wind clearing out the cobwebs. Ploughing was certainly more difficult than it is today, but you knew that if you were working with good horses they would make up for any of your shortcomings. It was a sort of team effort and you were aware of it. You see how much team effort you can get out of a tractor!'

The comradeship of working with horses was matched, it seems, by the comradeship of working with other skilled men; there was a sense of belonging among farm-workers generally, and in particular among the workers on particular farms – they would go around together, drinking and playing as a distinct group during the few hours of freedom they had each week. However, it wasn't all sweetness and light: some farmers and their foremen would quickly earn themselves a reputation as unreasonable or oppressive, and workers would go to them only as a last resort. Nevertheless, according to George such men were in a minority, and generally speaking if you pulled your weight you were among friends:

'Other workers would try to help you if they could, and they'd always be good with a new lad who'd perhaps never ploughed before because a lad's first day at the plough could be awful for him even if it was a bit of fun for the rest of the men – he'd be bound to get in a mess a few times. The solution on most farms was to give a new lad a pair of experienced horses to see him right, and he would never be expected to draw the first furrow across the field; that was always done by an experienced man, because the line set would be the line all the subsequent furrows followed – if the first was wrong, they'd all be wrong, and all the other ploughmen round about would soon know if so-and-so had made a bad job of a field. The art of the thing was to plough straight, and if you could do that you were doing well.'

Virtual self-sufficiency was an important aspect of life on a farm early in the twentieth century; thus the food the workers ate was produced on the farm, and farms would breed, train and work their own horses. 'All the farms on which I worked bred their own horses for farm work, though one or two would also breed them to be sold. One farm I worked on sold them to the brewers – all the brewers round about had teams of horses to pull the drays. They still keep horses to this day, but only for special occasions. And what few people know is that each brewer would only take horses of a particular colour, so Tetley would only ever have grey horses, for example, while Youngs insisted on black.'

In some parts of the country the practice was for farm horses to work right through the day without returning to their stables at midday. However, in George's part of Yorkshire the horses were always taken back to the stable at noon and fed before the men went in for the main meal of the day. 'We always fed the horses at midday like this and we got their feed ready for the night. After we'd finished our dinner, about one o'clock, we'd go out again and work through till about 7pm.'

Although the men had heard about the new tractors that were beginning to show up here and there in the 1930s, few had seen one, except perhaps as an exhibit at a show, and it was hard to imagine that tractors would ever really change the nature of land work for ever. 'There wasn't a single tractor round here,' said George, 'not one, they were unheard of, so far as I know. But we were too busy getting through the long days to worry much about them, or to imagine that they would ever make life easier for us.'

George was particularly busy at this time because, having started to work for the Vesteys, he was asked to take on the job of exercising a string of point-to-point horses, as well as continuing his work with the plough horses and waggons. 'I enjoyed that – they were fast and highly strung, and a marvellous ride. Vestey kept them as a hobby, though in fact they were valuable and he had some real champions among them. Of course as a farmworker I was never able to ride them in races, I only ever exercised them, but they were beautiful animals and it made a change from the heavy farm horses.

'I worked for the Vesteys from the age of eighteen to twenty-seven, and after what I'd gone through before on that farm owned by my relatives I have to say that the Vesteys were pretty good employers. When I left them I went as a stockman to Ampleforth College, the famous Catholic school between Kirby and Pickering; it was a huge place which owned two farms and a lot of land.

'At that time it was a tradition that wherever you worked on the land there was one week in the year when everyone, from the lowest ploughboy to the richest farmer, was allowed to have some fun: Martinmas, starting on November 23.' During Martimas week all the villages round the Dales held their annual sports days and dances. It was an age-old custom, and all the villagers, farmers and farm-workers from miles round about would look forward to it right through the year.

'A typical village sports day would start with athletics and pony racing, then in the evening there'd be a dance, and finally a singing competition. If you won the singing they gave you £5, which was a lot of money in those days. A friend and I had had a few singing lessons so we always had a bit of an advantage, but they tried to make it difficult by calling you up one by one and giving you a piglet to hold while you sang! The idea was that the pig would start struggling halfway through your song and put you off – and of course the audience would love that and roar with laughter!'

George was a great music lover, and as a young man he had the sort of musical talent that could have led to a complete change in career – he was so good that one year he won the singing competition at six consecutive village shows during Martinmas week. 'Everyone turned up at the singing competitions because only a few people had radios in those days; also there were no televisions, and musical entertainment was hard to come by. So lads and lasses biked in from miles round about, and the bookies did a roaring trade taking bets on who would win the races or the singing competitions.'

At the end of one competition, having won easily, George was approached by a man who offered to arrange to have him trained professionally in London. The stranger had been so impressed by the quality of George's voice that he was convinced the young man had a real future as a professional. 'I turned that offer down, though many said I was mad to do it. The main reason was that I couldn't bear the idea of living in a town; but I have to confess that sometimes I have a slight twinge of regret for what I might have turned out to be if I'd said yes!'

The singing competitions were so important in the Dales that large amounts of money were bet on who would win. And when the stakes were high, occasionally the unscrupulous showed up, as George explained: 'I remember once I was hot favourite to win, and just before I went on I had to go to the loo. I was standing there when a man sidled up to me and asked how much I wanted to bodge it. I said I wouldn't do it. I wanted to win, but he'd certainly have paid me a lot more than the £5 I got when I went out and won. I couldn't bear the idea of deliberately throwing the thing, even though I'd have done very well out of it. Anyway, I collected my £5 and then my friends and I set off for the pub and spent the lot.'

By the time he reached the Ampleforth College farms – 'two big dairy farms and 1,500 acres' – George had married, but fortunately the new job did not demand the long hours he had endured as a single man working with horses: 'At Ampleforth I looked after the young cattle mostly, and the sheep. What a lovely job it was, too – up at 7am, a wonderful little pony to ride round the fields, and I stopped work at 3.30pm, which was a bit more civilised than I was used to.

'I was tempted away from Ampleforth by money, and worked for a while in Cambridgeshire; it was a well paid job, but a real culture shock for me after spending my whole life in Yorkshire. I think they resented me, the local people I mean, because they considered a local man should have got the job; but the owners of the farm had decided that if they wanted a sheep man they'd be better to get him from sheep country, and that's how they got me. Anyway, I didn't stick it for long – I didn't like it, and my wife had a nervous breakdown over it. So I applied for a job at Askham Bryan College, an agricultural college back in my part of Yorkshire.'

This was the job that fashioned George into an acknowledged authority on sheep and sheep farming, although he learned the hard way – by trial and error and making mistakes, and by listening to others: 'A shepherd's life is a constant worry; for one thing, sheep are always getting themselves rigged – that's what we say up here when a sheep gets on its back – and because of the weight of the fleece they can't get up again; if they stay like that too long they blow up and die. You have to know what you're doing with sheep – they need moving regularly to fresh grazing on the right sort of pasture, and in winter they need adequate feed the whole time, particularly the in-lamb ewes.

'Lambing is the most demanding time; in the first place you must be careful not to put the ram to your ewes too early or your lambs will be born too early the following year, and then you can suffer heavy losses if the weather is cold or wet. We always aimed to lamb about mid-March when the worst of the weather would be over and there'd be grass already growing.

'We always had Scotch half-bred sheep both during my time at the college farms and earlier in Cambridgeshire.

At the college we would take the ewes into sheds and yards at lambing time, but if the weather was all right we had them out again in the fields within a day or so. That was a comparatively modern arrangement; in my early days, we had to get on and build a straw fold for lambing in the corner of a field, but the difference in the number of lost lambs wasn't that great so far as I recall. There were always plenty of farm-workers to call on for extra help – our record was eleven men working flat out through a day, and 89 lambs at the end of it. Later on, during my days at the college farms, it was all a lot easier because there were so many students to help.'

Like many good shepherds George bred and trained his own sheepdogs for decades, but he has always seen them as working animals, not pets. 'No, dogs were always too much a part of my working life for me to keep one now, just to have it about the place, and besides I'm too busy. Though I've retired I'm always out seeing friends and so on, and if I had a dog I'd have to cart it around with me or stay at home with it.

'When I worked full time as a shepherd, of course I had to have a dog. I used to breed and train my own – if you made a bit of a name for yourself as a trainer you could make money out of a well-trained sheepdog, good money. We used to sell them for £300–£400, but towards the end of my career a top dog might cost you £2,000. I used to go to Scotland and Northumberland looking for good dogs and often a man would come to me and ask me to find a dog for him.

'The working life of a sheepdog is only about five years and though they're difficult to train the big hurdle is your first dog; when you've trained that it's really just a question of repeating the trick and adapting things slightly to suit the temperament of the individual animal. Remember too that you're dealing with an animal that has been bred for generations to learn difficult tasks.'

With sheep, George had found an area of farming in which he was to prove particularly adept. Over the years he won a string of top prizes at the Great Yorkshire Show where latterly he was asked to judge the sheep classes. He never gave up his visits to the Great Yorkshire, but remembered clearly what a rare treat it was to go to a show, or anywhere for that matter, in the 1930s: 'We had no money, and no means of transport other than an old bike. We relied on the local shows for our entertainment, and in summer groups of us would walk round the neighbouring farms to see how well the other farm lads had done their work. Were the furrows straight? Were the fields clean, by which I mean weed-free? That's an important point, by the way. Modern farmers tell you that you need weed killers to get rid of weeds. Well, let me tell you, that's nonsense – we used skill, not chemicals, and our fields were good and clean. The trick was to harrow the field just as the weeds were coming up, in other words at their most vulnerable stage, and that would kill them right enough.'

For George, as for so many of those who worked on the land in the 1930s, the greatest changes in farming coincided with the start of the Second World War. Farmers were encouraged to use the new tractors, and ancient tracts of grassland were ploughed up everywhere. But farmers are a traditional lot and many clung to the old ways. They were torn between the desire for high efficiency and for continuity: 'It is certainly true that even as the horses began to disappear people began to miss them; compared to a tractor they were so marvellous to work with. With a tractor the pleasure went out of it overnight.

'All right, you had to learn how to maintain the thing, how to get it started in cold weather and so on, but that was nothing compared to the years we spent and the trouble we went to with a young horse. There was a lot of skill and patience involved in making a good job of breaking in a horse, which really started when the foal was only about a week old, when a halter would be put on, and it would be led gently around. You'd get it used to that, but then you'd more or less leave it until it was two. With the two-year-olds you'd put on what we called breaking tackle, a bit and so on; some took to it well from the outset, others might take a bit longer, but it was very rare to get a thoroughly bad, untrainable animal. You'd start to get them used to the reins, then to being harnessed alongside another horse. It was all done gently and gradually, because generations of horsemen had found that that was the best way. Finally you'd put a young horse in the shafts, and usually it would soon settle down and learn the ropes.'

Few farm horses were deliberately malicious, though they might kick if they were frightened and a kick from a Shire could, and occasionally did, kill. A grown horse might weigh a ton, and it might injure a man without even being aware of it: 'I remember once I was trapped by a horse in the stable. We'd driven a very flighty young 'un into the stable between two older quieter ones which calmed it down, then I went in against the side of the stall and the big old horse just leaned on me, thinking I was the wall, I suppose – that's all it did, there was no kicking or deliberate mischief, but it was enough to break half my ribs! I stood there half crushed and unable to breathe while the horse hadn't a clue it was doing anything wrong. I realised I was in trouble, but eventually managed to slide down the wall even as she pinned me there, and I got out by crawling round her feet.

'The horses had lovely names, I remember – Cobby, Duke, Blossom, Violet, Royal and Smartie – but we weren't sentimental about them. When they were too old to work we called in the knacker because you couldn't afford to give a horse a retirement out at grass.'

This lack of sentimentality was undoubtedly grounded in the simple fact that, at least until the 1930s, horses were everywhere, and they were purely functional animals. For example the railway station in York had about sixty horses at any one time, fed and stabled by the railway board and used to deliver the myriad goods that arrived by rail. The milk delivery companies had dozens of ponies, so too the coal merchants, the grocers, the fire and ambulance services.

George's love of horses stayed with him; in his latter years he owned a pony and trap which he drove round the lanes near his home with his daughter Georgina, a lawyer who practised in Harrogate and of whom he was intensely proud. 'She's a marvellous girl,' he says with a twinkle, 'but I can't imagine where she got her brains. Can't have been from me! Mind you, I always used to say to her "Don't be too proud to tell your friends your father was a shepherd!"'

But if George was proud of the old farming skills, he was also aware that in the details of everyday existence, life was once very hard and that whatever the disadvantages of modern living, most country people are better off in the modern world than they were in the past.

'Oh, it was unimaginable by today's standards. Just take clothing – a working man had a thick heavy pair of corduroy trousers made each year, usually in that week off at Martinmas I told you about, and those would have to last him at least a year. None of this business of having a change of clothes – you needed money to have that. I had one pair of trousers, and that was it.

'When he was taken on by a farmer and they had agreed his hiring fee for the year, a man knew he would only be paid at the end of that year. He'd not get a penny till then, except in exceptional circumstances, so he only had the money for new trousers – or anything else for that matter – when Martinmas came round again. It was the same with boots. He'd get himself a big pair of hobnails, hand-made of course, and they'd have to last a twelve-month. Also, every man wore a waistcoat then and a hat; you wouldn't dare be seen out without a hat at one time.'

One of George's greatest friends was Geoffrey Berridge. Like George, he was very conscious of the skills and adaptability required to make a good farmworker. 'In the old days he had to turn his hand to just about anything, not like the factory worker who does his one little job and that's all. The farm-worker couldn't say "Oh, I can't do that!" If he was told to do it, he'd do it, whether it was ploughing, harrowing, hedging, ditching, thatching, reaping or sowing. That's what it meant to be on the land. And you were proud of what you did – that's why horse brasses and other harness ornamentation were so important, because a horseman was very proud of his animals and his calling. But that long tradition has gone completely now, except in the memories of old men like us.'

Geoffrey may remember the skills demanded of the farm-worker in those far-off days, but he also remembered some of the petty aspects of relationships between man and master. 'Well, when you sat down to dinner with the farm foreman there was a tradition that if you were having pie – and we were nearly always having pie! – you each cut your own piece, but you never cut right into the middle of the thing. The reason was that when all the men had eaten, there would be the best bit of pie left in the middle of the dish for the foreman; it was his perk, and he guarded it jealously. And you weren't allowed to speak a single word during dinner, not one – I spoke once and was growled at by the boss. You also had to stop eating the very minute the foreman stopped, so if you had any sense you ate up pretty sharpish.

'And on the rare occasions when you could have a bath, and you were lucky if that was once a week, a tub would be filled with hot water and six or seven men would wash in it one after the other in order of seniority. Imagine that happening today! Generally speaking we never saw hot water – when you came in from the fields you just sat down and ate. No one thought anything of it.

INDEX

YESTERDAY'S FARM
Valerie Porter
ISBN: 978-0-7153-2878-1

Find out about rural life in this spellbinding journey back to the farmsteads and fields of the last century.

THE BOOK OF FORGOTTEN CRAFTS
Paul Felix Siân Ellis and Tom Quinn
ISBN: 978-0-7153-3831-5

This title reveals the fascinating history of British craftsmanship in a series of interviews with leading crafters at work in Britain today.

JAM TOMORROW
Tom Quinn
ISBN: 978-0-2764-4504-0

Offers a captivating social history of post-war Britain, from 1945-1951, through hundreds of previously unpublished interviews and stunning photography.